ISLAM VIS-A-VIS HINDU TEMPLES

Hindu Temples: What Happened to Them,
— Volume I, *A Preliminary Survey*, by Arun Shourie and others
— Volume II, *The Islamic Evidence*, by Sita Ram Goel

ISLAM VIS-A-VIS HINDU TEMPLES

SITA RAM GOEL

VOICE OF INDIA
NEW DELHI

First published 1993
First reprint 2000

ISBN 81-85990-06-9

Published by Voice of India, 2/18, Ansari Road, New Delhi–110 002 and printed at Rajkamal Electric Press, Delhi – 110 033.

CONTENTS

PREFACE

A court order in 1986 threw open for Hindu worship the gates of the temple-turned-mosque at the Rāmajanmabhūmi site in Ayodhya. Hindus were overjoyed, and started looking forward to the coming up of a grand Rāma Mandira at the sacred spot. But they were counting without the stalwarts of Secularism in the Nehruvian establishment. It was not long before a hysterical cry was heard — "Secularism in danger!"

The Marxist–Muslim combine launched a two-pronged campaign. On the one hand, they proclaimed that Muslims had destroyed no Hindu temples except those few which were stinking with hoarded wealth or had become centres of local rebellions, and that Islam as a religion was never involved in iconoclasm. On the other hand, they accused the Hindus of destroying any number of Buddhist, Jain and Animist shrines in the pre-Islamic past.

As a student of India's history, ancient as well as medieval, I could see quite clearly that they were playing the Goebbelsian game of the Big Lie. But they could not be countered because they had come to dominate the academia and control the mass media during the heyday of the Nehru dynasty. Most of the prestigious press was owned by Hindu moneybags. But they had placed their papers in the hands of the most brazen-faced Hindu-baiters.

The most unkindest cut of all, however, came from the Vishva Hindu Parishad and the Bharatiya Janata Party. They were doing nothing towards debunking Secularist lies about Hinduism vis-a-vis Buddhism, Jainism, and Animism. But they were trumpeting from the house-tops that Islam did not permit the destruction of other people's places of worship, and that *namāz* offered in a mosque built on the site of a temple was not acceptable to Allāh! They were laying the blame for the destruction of the Rāma Mandir not on Islam as an ideology of terror but on Bābur as a foreign invader! One wondered whether this kowtowing to Islam was prompted by ignorance, or cowardice, or calculation, or a combination of them all. The Islam of which the Hindu leaders were talking was to be found neither in the Qu'rān nor in the Sunnah of the Prophet.

The only ray of light in this encircling gloom was Arun Shourie, the veteran journalist and the Chief Editor of the *Indian Express* at that time. On February 5, 1989, he frontpaged an article, *Hideaway Communalism*, showing that while the Urdu version of a book by Maulana

Hakim Sayid Abdul Hai of the Nadwatul-Ulama at Lucknow had admitted that seven famous mosques had been built on the sites of Hindu temples, the English translation published by the Maulana's son, Abul Hasan Ali Nadwi (Ali Mian), had eschewed the "controversial passages". He also published in the *Indian Express* three articles written by me on the subject of Islamic iconoclasm. This was a very courageous defiance of the ban imposed by Islam and administered by Secularism, namely, that crimes committed by Islam cannot even be whispered in private, not to speak of being proclaimed in public.

Finally, VOICE OF INDIA published Volume I of a projected series — *Hindu Temples: What Happened to Them* — in April, 1991. It was a collection of relevant articles by Arun Shourie, Harsh Narain, Jay Dubashi, Ram Swarup, and myself. An important part of the volume was a list of 2000 Muslim monuments built on the sites and/or with the materials of Hindu temples. This list became famous all over the country and even abroad as soon as it came out.

Meanwhile, the evidence I had collected regarding Islamic iconoclasm could already cover several, and much bigger, volumes. VOICE OF INDIA published Volume II of the series in May, 1991. It was devoted exclusively to Islamic evidence, historical as well theological, and was received very well, particularly by the world of scholarship. Only the prestigious newspapers and periodicals in this country ignored it completely; they did not even acknowledge it in their "Books Received" column. An extensive review, however, was written by the Belgian scholar, Koenraad Elst. This review was published by VOICE OF INDIA in 1992 under the title *Negationism in India: Concealing the Record of Islam.*

The following chapters have been extracted from the second and enlarged edition of Volume II of *Hindu Temples: What Happened to Them,* which has been published recently. The purpose of this small publication is to focus attention on the stark fact that the destruction of other peoples places of worship is a pious performance in Islam, after the precendent set by the Prophet himself when he destroyed all pre-Islamic pagan temples in Arabia. The Qu'rān also sanctions iconoclasm in very clear terms.

Hindus have to realize that their temples are not safe so long as they recognize Islam as a religion and thus permit it to retain its self-righteous aggressiveness. When the Temple of Somnath was rebuilt in post-independence India, the following Urdu couplet started circulating among the Muslims of this country:

mandar tō sōmnāth kā ta'mīr hō gāyā
ik aur ghaznavī kī faqat intizār hai

(The temple of Somnath has been rebuilt. We now wait for another Mahmūd Ghaznavi.)

People who cherish the illusion that Muslims can be persuaded to make concessions if Islam is flattered, live in a fool's paradise. The whole history of Islam in this country and elsewhere is a witness that Muslims have never made a concession to the *kafirs*, particularly when it came to the essentials of their creed. It is not Allāh but the Prophet who sits at the heart of Islam and dictates its doings. Muslims cannot compromise when it concerns the Sunnah of the Prophet which they regard as the divinely inspired model for all time to come.

Hindus will do well to learn from the experience of Mahatma Gandhi. He spent a life-time in singing hymns of praise to the "noble faith of Islam", and extolling the Qu'rān and the Prophet. He championed the cause of Khilafat as dearer than that of the freedom for India. He believed sincerely that the only solution of the "communal problem" in India was to concede to the Muslims whatever they demanded. And yet he was regarded by a majority of the Muslims as the "greatest enemy of Islam", and abused as such in the foulest language by the Urdu press. He lived to see the holocaust of Partition caused by Islam. His only fault was that, unlike the votaries of Secularism, he was proud of being a Hindu.

The leaders of the movement which passes as the Hindu movement at present have been very critical, and rightly so, of the Mahatma's policy vis-a-vis Islam. But instead of learning any lesson from the Mahatma's folly, they are getting more and more inclined towards following the same path, namely, flattery of Islam in the hope of obtaining concessions from it. The present-day Hindu leaders are nowhere near the Mahatma when it comes to being convinced, conscious, and proud Hindus. Nor is their praise of Islam as sincere as it was in the case of the Mahatma. They are flattering Islam as a matter of strategy, and thus committing the double sin of stupidity and craftiness. They are most likely to land Hindu society into a situation from which it may not be able to find a way out.

Islam has been tormenting Hindu society for more than thirteen hundred years. It has inflicted no end of grievous injuries on the Hindu homeland, Hindu population, and the Hindu heritage. It is high time that Hindus stop whining about and weeping over the Muslim behaviour pattern, and try to understand the system of belief from which the pattern follows. The problem before the Hindus is not Muslims but Islam. Muslims are our own people whom Islam has alienated from us to the extent that they repudiate even their ancestry. Hindus have so far failed to study Islam from its orthodox sources. In fact, they have been more than willing to buy the fairy tales which the salesmen of Islam have fabricated, particularly about the Prophet, the Pious Caliphs, and the Sūfīs. What is worse, Hindus have allowed Islam to impose an emergency on this country so that Islam can be praised but not examined even in terms of normal human reason and natural human morality. That will not do. Hindus have to go much farther and process Islam in terms of their own spiritual vision derived from the Vedas, the Itihāsa-Purāṇa, and the Dharmaśāstras. Then alone they will know what Islam is. I have not the slightest doubt that what passes for Hindu tolerance vis-a-vis Islam is no more than a combination of ignorance and cowardice.

New Delhi
May 27, 1993

SITA RAM GOEL

Chapter One

ISLAMIC ICONOCLASM IN INDIA

Commenting on the history of Central Asia, Heinrich Zimmer writes: "During the sixth and early seventh centuries AD the whole tract was controlled by Turkish rulers, but in the course of the seventh, with increasing strength of the T'ang Emperors, China gained control. Finally, however, under the onslaught of Islam, from the eighth century to the tenth, both Buddhist and Manichaean as well as the Nestorian Christian culture and monuments of the region were destroyed."[1]

Coming to North India, he continues: "In the north very little survives of the ancient edifices that were there prior to the Muslim conquest: only a few mutilated religious sites remain[2].... It is clear from Indian literature that both temples and images must have existed in the second century BC and perhaps earlier. Very little architectural evidence remains, however, antedating the epoch of the Gupta dynasty (c. AD 320–650), for it was precisely in the Ganges Valley, the central and chief area of the Gupta empire, that the Muslim empire flourished a millennium later and most of the monuments above ground were destroyed by the sectarian zeal of Islam. The oldest stone ruins that have been found represent not the beginnings of a style, but fully developed forms."[3]

He is specific about the destruction of Buddhism in India. "Since the earliest important body of Indian art surviving to us," he says, "stems from the century of Aśoka, it is pre-dominantly Buddhist. During subsequent periods, however, Buddhist and Hindu (Brahmanical) themes alternate in rich profusion. The two traditions flourished side by side, even sharing colleges and monasteries, for nearly two millenniums, until about the height of the Muslim conquest (c. AD 1200), Buddhism disappeared from the land of its birth."[4]

By now there are hundreds of publications which provide detailed studies of the architecture and sculpture of many Hindu monuments from all over India. But only a few of them, mostly written by foreigners, state clearly that what have been studied are heaps of ruins dug out by archaeologists from under tell-tale mounds. Hindu writers, by and

---

[1] Heinrich Zimmer, *Art of Indian Asia*, Princeton, Paperback Edition, 1983, Vol. I, p. 201.

[2] Ibid., p. 246.

[3] Ibid., p. 270.

[4] Ibid., p. 5n.,

large, leave the impression as if they have studied monuments which stand intact and in all their original majesty. It is only when we come to the plates that the truth dawns upon us. What we find there staring us in the face are mostly ruins with architectural fragments and mutilated sculptures lying scattered on the surface or brought up from underneath.

The travels of Buddhist pilgrims from China and the pre-Islamic epigraphic records on stones and copper plates tell us how many temples and monasteries stood at what place and at what time. Histories written by medieval Muslim historians inform us as to who made these monuments disappear and when. The two sources, taken together, present a total picture which historians have so far studied in separate parts.

Hindus are famous (or notorious) for their poor sense of history as Christians, Muslims and the modern Westerners understand it. Hindus of medieval India were no exception. They have left no detailed record of what happened to their places of worship and pilgrimage at the hands of Islamic iconoclasm. We do come across descriptions of the Muslim behaviour pattern in the Hindu literature from that period. An invariable ingredient of that pattern is the destruction of temples and the desecration of idols. Accounts relating to destruction of particular temples at particular dates and places are very rare. That sort of detailed evidence comes almost entirely from medieval Muslim sources, literary and epigraphic. Archaeological explorations and excavations in modern times have only confirmed and supplemented that evidence.

Times have changed and so also some moral standards of mankind. Religious tolerance is a value which is cherished today universally by the dominant intellectual elite of the world. Muslim theologians, scholars and politicians in present-day India, therefore, want us to believe that Islam stands for religious tolerance and that there was never a time when it interfered by means of force with the religious beliefs or practices of other people. They resent any reference whatsoever to the destruction of Hindu temples by Muslim invaders and rulers in medieval India. Leftist professors and politicians who subscribe to what they describe as Secularism, dismiss this significant chapter in medieval India's history as a canard spread by "Hindu communalists". As most of these worthies happen to be Hindus by accident of birth, they add considerable weight to Muslim assertions.

There was, however, a time not so long ago when Muslim theologians prescribed and Muslim swordsmen practised the destruction of

Hindu temples[5] on a large scale. Hundreds of Muslim historians have credited their heroes with what they rightly regarded as a pious performance according to the principal tenets of Islam. Most of these histories, written in India as well as elsewhere in the Islamic world, have been printed and translated in one or more of the modern languages. They exist in cold print on the shelves of public and private libraries all over the world. Then there are inscriptions in Arabic and Persian which proclaim the destruction of Hindu temples or their conversion into mosques with considerable pride. These, too, have been deciphered, translated and published by archaeological surveys covering India, Central Asia, Eastern Iran, Afghanistan, Pakistan and Bangladesh. They leave us in no doubt about one of the favourite pastimes of pious Muslim princes in all these countries which constituted at one time the vast cradle of Hindu culture.

There are many Muslim monuments all over India which provide unmistakable evidence that materials from demolished Hindu temples have been used in their construction. Most of them carry inscriptions in Arabic or Persian stating when they were built and by whom. Some of these inscriptions proclaim that the mosques in which they stand installed, occupy the sites of Hindu temples which were destroyed. Others say that temple materials were used in the construction of the mosques. Similar inscriptions on stone slabs lying loose or not *in situ* have been discovered in many places. And it is a safe bet that many more inscriptions which refer to destruction of Hindu temples and construction of mosques etc., remain undiscovered or undeciphered or unpublished. Epigraphists entrusted with the decipherment of Arabic and Persian inscriptions have invariably been Muslims. Small wonder that they have been more than slow in presenting evidence which does not add glory to Islam in the eyes of modern men. Epigraphists in Secular India have been still less keen or scrupulous in searching and publishing evidence which compromises the picture of this country as a "haven of communal amity and peace before the advent of the British".

Islamic literary sources provide far more extensive evidence of temple destruction by the Muslim invaders of India in medieval times. They also cover a larger area, from Sinkiang and Transoxiana in the North to Tamil Nadu in the South, and from the Seistan province of present-day Iran in the West to Assam in the East. As we wade through

---

[5] The word "Hindu" has been used throughout this book to denote all schools of Sanātana Dharma — Brahmanical, Buddhist, and Jain. In our own times, however, the words "Hindu" and "Hinduism" have been made to mean what they never meant.

this evidence, we can visualise how this vast area, which was for long the cradle of Hindu culture, came to be literally littered with the ruins of temples and monasteries belonging to all schools of Sanātana Dharma—Bauddha, Jaina, Śaiva, Śākta, Vaishṇava and the rest. Archaeological explorations and excavations in modern times have proved unmistakably that most of the mosques, *mazārs*, *ziārats* and *dargāhs* which were built in this area in medieval times, stood on the sites of and were made from the materials of deliberately demolished Hindu monuments.

Hundreds of medieval Muslim historians who flourished in India and elsewhere in the world of Islam, have written detailed accounts of what their heroes did in various parts of the extensive Hindu homeland as they were invaded one after another. We have had access only to a few of these histories on account of our limitations in terms of language and resources. Most of the histories pertaining to what are known as provincial Muslim dynasties, have remained beyond our reach. One thing, however, becomes quite clear from the evidence we have been able to compile, namely, that almost all Muslim rulers destroyed or desecrated Hindu temples whenever and wherever they could. Archaeological evidence from various Muslim monuments, particularly mosques and *dargāhs*, not only confirms the literary evidence but also adds the names of some Muslim rulers whom Muslim historians have failed to credit with this pious performance.

SUMMING UP

Starting with Al-Bilādhurī who wrote in Arabic in the second half of the ninth century, and coming down to Syed Mahmudul Hasan who wrote in English in the eighth decade of the twentieth, we have cited from eighty histories and twenty-six inscriptions spanning a period of more than twelve hundred years. Our citations mention sixty-one kings, sixty-three military commanders and fourteen sufis who destroyed Hindu temples in one hundred and fifty-four localities, spread from Khurasan in the West to Tripura in the East, and from Transoxiana in the North to Tamil Nadu in the South, over a period of eleven hundred years. In most cases the destruction of temples was followed by erection of mosques, *madrasas* and *khānqāhs* etc., on the temple sites and, frequently, with temple materials. Allāh was thanked every time for enabling the iconoclast concerned to render service to the religion of Muhammad by means of this pious performance.[6]

[6] See *Hindu Temples: What Happened to Them*, Volume II, *The Islamic Evidence*, Voice of India, New Delhi, 1993.

Some more kings or commanders or sūfis who figure in these histories in a similar context may have remained unmentioned because we had access to the full texts only in a few cases; most of the time we had to remain content with excerpts or summaries made by modern historians in one context or the other. Many more localities have remained unspecified because quite often the histories under reference, instead of naming particular places, mention provinces and regions where large-scale destruction of temples took place as a result of general orders issued to this effect, or intensive campaigns undertaken for this purpose alone.

It is seldom that translations retain the full flavour of the language and meaning of the original works. In our case, some of the flavour must have been lost in citations which we had to translate into English from Urdu or Hindi renderings of the Persian texts. Even so, we feel that, taken together, the citations do bring out something of the religious zeal harboured by the historians concerned when they sat down to glorify Islam and highlight its heroes.

Coming to the heroes themeselves, some of them figure more prominently or frequently in our citations, such as Muhammad bin Qāsim, Mahmūd of Ghazni, Shamsu'd-Dīn Iltutmish, Alāu'd-Dīn Khaljī, Fīrūz Shāh Tughlaq, Ahmad Shāh I and Mahmūd Begḍhā of Gujarat, Sikander Lodī, and Aurangzeb; they have earned permanent fame in the annals of Islam by doing what they did to Hindus in general and to Hindu temples in particular. But the others, too, do not come out discreditably if a state of mind or an expressed intention is any indication. Maybe, their achievements in this context have found a more detailed description in histories to which we have had no access.

It is highly doubtful if the Mughal period deserves the credit that has been given to it as a period of religious tolerance. Akbar is now known only for his policy of *sulh-i-kul*, at least among the learned Hindus. It is no more remembered that to start with he was also a pious Muslim who had viewed as *jihād* his sack of Chittor. Nor is it understood by the learned Hindus that his policy of *sulh-i-kul* was motivated mainly by his bid to free himself from the stranglehold of the orthodox *'Ulamā*, and that any benefit which Hindus derived from it was no more than a by-product. Akbar never failed to demand daughters of the Rajput kings for his harem. Moreover, as our citations show, he was not able to control the religious zeal of his functionaries at the lower levels so far as Hindu temples were concerned. Jahāngīr, like many other Muslim kings, was essentially a wine-and-women loving person. He, however, became a pious Muslim when it came to Hindu temples of which he destroyed quite a few. Shāh Jahān did not hide what he wanted to do to the Hindus and their places of worship. His Islamic record on this score was much better than that of Jahāngīr. The reversal of Akbar's policy thus started by his two immediate successors reached its apotheosis in the reign of Aurangzeb, the paragon of Islamic piety in the minds of India's Muslims. What is more significant, Akbar has never been forgiven by those who have regarded themselves as custodians of Islam, right upto our own times; Maulana Abul Kalam Azad is a typical example. In any case, one swallow has never made a summer.

Certain localities also figure more prominently or more frequently in our citations, such as Multan, Thanesar, Kangra, Mathura, Somnath, Varanasi, Ujjain, Chidambaram, Puri, Dwarka, Girinar and Kanchipuram. The iconoclasts paid special attention to temples in these places or mounted repeated attacks on them. They knew that these were the holy cities of the Hindus, and entertained the fond hope that desecration of idols and destruction of temples in these sanctuaries was most likely to make the Hindus lose faith in their "false gods" and prepare them for receiving the "light of Islam". That, however, does not mean that destruction of temples at other places was in any sense less thorough. Our citations reveal more or less the same pattern everywhere, once the swordsmen of Islam got fired by their religious fervour.

It was not unoften that Hindu temples were admired by the iconoclasts for their strength, or antiquity, or exquisiteness, or the expense incurred on their construction. We are told that they were "as firm as the faith of the faithful" and "a thousand years old". It was estimated that they must have cost so many "thousand thousand dirhams" or so many "lakhs of asharfies". But none of these plus points was reason enough for sparing them from the fate they deserved according to the Sunnah of the Prophet. They embodied an "age of darkness and error", they housed "false gods", and they enticed people away from the worship of the "one and only true God" — Allāh of the Qur'ān.

So the temples were attacked "all along the way" as the armies of Islam advanced; they were "robbed of their sculptural wealth", "pulled down", "laid waste", "burnt with naptha", "trodden under horse's hoofs", and "destroyed from their very foundations", till "not a trace of them remained". Mahmūd of Ghazni robbed and burnt down 1,000 temples at Mathura, and 10,000 in and around Kanauj. One of his successors, Ibrāhīm, demolished 1,000 temples each in Hindustan (Ganga–Yamuna Doab) and Malwa. Muhammad Ghūrī destroyed another 1,000 at Varanasi. Qutbu'd-Dīn Aibak employed elephants for pulling down 1,000 temples in Delhi. 'Alī I 'Ādil Shāh of Bijapur destroyed 200 to 300 temples in Karnataka. A sufi, Qāyim Shāh, destroyed 12 temples at Tiruchirapalli. Such exact or approximate counts, however, are available only in a few cases. Most of the time we are informed that "many strong temples which would have remained unshaken even by the trumpets blown on the Day of Judgment, were levelled with the ground when swept by the wind of Islām".

We find the Muslim historians going into raptures as they describe scenes of desecration and destruction. For Amīr Khusrū it was always an occasion to show off the power of his poetic imagination. When Jalālu'd-Dīn Khaljī wrought havoc at Jhain, "A cry rose from the temples as if a second Mahmūd had taken birth". The temples in the environs of Delhi were "bent in prayers" and "made to do prostration", by Alāu'd-Dīn Khaljī. When the temple of Somnath was destroyed and its debris thrown into the sea towards the west, the poet rose to his full height. "So the temple of Somnāth," he wrote, "was made to bow towards the Holy Mecca, and the temple lowered its head and jumped into the sea, so you may say that the building first said its prayers and then had a bath."

Our citations have a lot to tell about how the votaries of Islam viewed the idols of Gods and Goddesses enshrined in the temples. Though the Arabic word used in the Qur'ān for idols is *ṣanam*, we find our historians using the word *but* which they had borrowed form the Persians. The Persian word was a corruption of the Sanskrit word "*Buddha*", with which the Persians had been famillar for a long time because there were many Buddhist temples in Seistan, Khurasan and Transoxiana. The word "*budd*" has actually been used in some of the histories when referring to idols which were burnt or which the infidels were prevented from worshipping. Small wonder that the temples which enshrined statues of the Buddha became special targets for the Islamic iconoclasts. We shall deal with this subject in greater detail in another study; for now, it is sufficient to say that the death-blow to Buddhism, a religion centred round temples and monasteries and monks, was delivered by the armies of Islam and not by the much-maligned "Brahmanical reaction" as our Marxist "historians" are never tired of telling the world.

There was, however, one name which intrigued the iconoclasts for a long time, till the matter was cleared by some scholars of Islam in consultation with the Brahmans. It seems that the Arabs were familiar with the word "*Somanātha*" (which they pronounced as "Somnāt") even in the pre-Islamic period. Arab merchants who visited or lived in Gujarat must have told their countrymen about this fabulous Śiva temple. It is also quite likely that Somnath was a place of pilgrimage for the pre-Islamic Arabs who were "idolaters" like the Hindus and could not but have felt reverence for "Somnāt". Something of this reverence seems to have survived even after Islam brought about a radical transformation in their religious values. We find reflection of it in the story that *Manāt*, a Goddess of the pagan Arabs, had escaped when the Prophet tried to destroy her, and taken refuge in the temple of "Somnāt"; the word "Somnāt" was split into "So" and "manāt" in order to support the story. We find references to this story in several histories. Once in a while another Arab Goddess, Lāt, was also suspected to be hiding at Somnath after escaping the wrath of Muhammad.

In any case, the Qur'ān had proclaimed that the idols were "deaf and dumb", could "neither help nor harm", and "did not know it when they were broken". Subsequent theologians extended the meaning of "broken" and explained that the idols did not know when they were robbed of their adornments or defiled or mutilated; their only function was to "deceive" those who had not been blessed by the "message of monotheism". So a Muslim iconoclast cut off the hands of a Hindu idol in Seistan and plucked out its eyes in order to demonstrate the "divine truth". Muhammad bin Qāsim took off the necklace of the idol at Multan and replaced it with a piece of cow's flesh. The idol did not "protest", nor did it do anything else in order to prove that it had any "power for good or evil". Other veterans of Islam tried other methods to show to the "infidels" that their "gods" were "helpless" and they themselves "misguided".

Again, we can depend upon the poetic powers of Amīr Khusrū. He quoted the Qur'ān before describing the iconoclasm at Somnath. "It seemed," he worte, "as if the tongue of the Imperial sword explained the meaning of the text: 'So he (Abraham) broke them (the idols) into pieces except the chief of them, that haply they may return to it.' Such a pagan country, the Mecca of the infidels, now became the Medina of Islam." The earliest historians relate that while Mahmūd broke the other idols, he carried the main "idol" unbroken to Ghazni. So the "big brother" did not know what had happened to the "little ones", as in the story of Abraham in the Qur'ān.[7] Khusrū's highest poetic performance, however, came when he described the scene at Chidambaram. "The

[7]Qu'rān, 21.51-70.

stone idol called Ling Mahadeo," he sang, "which had been a long time established at that place and on which the women of the infidels rubbed their vaginas for (sexual) satisfaction, these upto this time the kick of the horse of Islam had not attempted to break...The Musalmans destroyed all the *lings* and Deo Narain fell down, and the other gods who had fixed their seats there raised their feet, and jumped so high, that at one leap they reached the fort of Lanka, and in that affright the *lings* themselves would have fled had they any legs to stand on."

To resume the story, some of the idols were made of precious metals and/or adorned with costly jewels; they had to be handled with care so that the faithful were not deprived of the booty promised by Allāh to those who removed his rivals out of the way. Such idols were first divested of their jewellery, then they were broken or burnt, and finally melted down; the bullion and the jewels were forwarded to the caliph or the king, whoever happened to be the patron of the "holy expedition". Occasionally, the idols were simply collected and sent to the capital city and it was the despot there who decided what to do with them. They certainly provided "great fun" to the "chosen people" before being disposed off in whatever manner was found appropriate, depending upon the type of the idols. Those made of precious metals ended in the royal treasury. Those made of inferior metals were turned into various instruments or vessels or used for decorative purposes such as door handles; later on, the bigger ones were recast to make cannon. Idols made of wood and stone etc., were broken and scattered on the doorsteps of mosques, particularly the Jāmi' Masjids, so that people on their way to prayers could trample or cleanse their soiled feet upon them, before entering the "sacred precincts" for "offering prayers to Allah" and "glorifying his last Prophet".

Several instances are cited when the Hindus tried to ransom their idols, sometimes by expressing willingness to pay their weight in gold. All such offers were "rejected with contempt" because the hero concerned wanted to earn "merit in the eyes of Allāh" rather than "mere mammon". Mahmūd of Ghazni made the point when he said at Somnath that he wanted to be known as a *but-shikan* (idol-breaker) and not as a *but-farosh* (idol-seller) when Allah called his name on the Day of Judgement. Those who want to explain away the destruction of Hindu temples in terms of economic motives, are called upon to explain these instances.

Mahmūd of Ghazni broke many idols with his own hand, including that of "Somnāt". He sent the pieces to Mecca, Medina and Baghdad, besides keeping some in his own capital at Ghazni. It was not for nothing that his coins struck at Lahore described him as *"but-shikan"*, idol-breaker. Subsequent sultāns followed his example. Unfortunately for them, the "accursed Mangol", Changiz Khān, overran a large part of Islamdom and blocked the way to the "holy cities" in the first quarter of the thirteenth century, just at the time when a vast field for breaking idols and collecting their pieces was opening before the heroes of Islam in Hind. In AD 1258, his grandson, Halākū, beat their own idol, the Caliph, into pulp and got the "holy" city of Baghdad ploughed over. So the pieces had perforce to lie before mosques in lesser places—Lahore, Multan, Delhi, Lakhnauti, Daulatabad, Gulbarga, Madura, Burhanpur, Bidar, Mandu, Ahmadabad, Jaunpur, Agra, Ahmadnagar, Bijapur, Golkonda, Hyderabad, Aurangabad. They were brought in by cart-loads in the time of Aurangzeb. One of our historians tells us that 'Alī I 'Ādil Shāh of Bijapur broke four to five thousand idols with his own hands while campaigning in Karnataka.

Meanwhile, other methods of telling the "truth" about the idols had been devised by the more imaginative among the swordsmen of Islam. Fīrūz Shāh Tughlaq had the idol at Purī perforated for passing ropes through it and dragged it along the road to Delhi. The pieces of the idol at Kangra were given by him to the butchers for being used as weights while selling meat. The copper umberlla of the same idol he got recast into pots for heating water with which the faithful washed their "hands, feet and faces" before saying their prayers. Mahmūd Khaljī of Malwa had the idol at Kumbhalgadh reduced to lime which was put in *pans* (betel-leaves) and the Hindus were forced to "eat their god". He had taken literally a latter-day story of what Mahmūd of Ghazni had done to the idol of "Somnāt" when the Brahmans arrived in his capital to "ransom their god".

The Brahmans who were custodians of the "idols and idol-houses", and "teachers of the infidels", also received their share of attention from the soldiers of Allāh. Our citations contain only stray references to the Brahmans because they have been compiled primarily with reference to the destruction of temples. Even so, they provide the broad contours of another chapter in the history of medieval India, a chapter which has yet to be brought out in full. The Brahmans are referred to as "magicians" by some Islamic invaders and massacred straight away. Elsewhere, the Hindus who are not totally defeated and want to surrender on some terms, are made to sign a treaty saying that the Brahmans will be expelled from the temples. The holy cities of the Hindus were "the nests of the Brahmans" who had to be slaughtered before or after the destruction of temples, so that these places were "cleansed" completely of *"kufr"* and made fit as "abodes of Islam".

Amīr Khusrū describes with great glee how the heads of Brahmans "danced from their necks and fell to the ground at their feet", along with those of the other "infidels" whom Malik Kāfūr had slaughtered during the sack of the temples at Chidambaram. Fīrūz Shāh Tughlaq got bags filled with cow's flesh, tied them round the necks of Brahmans, and had these "mines of *kufr* and *shirk*" paraded through his army camp at Kangra. Muhmūd Shāh II Bahmanī bestowed on himself the honour of being a *ghāzi* by killing in cold blood the helpless Brāhmaṇa priests of the local temple after Hindu warriors had died fighting in defence of the fort at Kondapalli. The present-day progressives, leftists and *dalits* whose main plank is anti-Brahminism have no reason to feel innovative about their ideology. Anti-Brahminism in India is as old as the advent of Islam. Our present-day Brahmin-baiters have to be told that they are no more than the ideological descendants of the Islamic invaders.

The next step which the heroes of Islam took after a place had ben "purged by the sword form the filth of impurity and the thorn of god-plurality" and the "foundations of infidelity destroyed", was to build mosques and *madrasas* etc., on the same sites where the temples stood, most often with the materials of those very temples. The operation was generally preceded by a pious ritual in which the victors prostrated themselves and praised Allāh "for the honour He bestows on Islām and the Musalmāns". Cows were slaughtered on the temple sites in order to render them unclean for the Hindus for all time to come; it had been noticed that the Hindus demolished the mosques and rebuilt their temples on the same sites whenever they recaptured a place. Now the mosques and *madrasas* could spread the "light of Islam" without interruption. Finally, the "servants of Allah" took over—the *khatībs,* the *mu'zzins,* the *muhtahsibs* and the *qāzīs*. The "uproar of the heathens gave way to shouts of *Allahū Akbar*" and the "strongholds of heathenism were made into abodes of Islām". Meanwhile, the endowments enjoyed by the temples had been transferred to the upcoming Islamic establishments, so that whatever temple priests had survived the slaughter had to starve while the Muslim clerics prospered.

The most significant feature of our histories, however, is the religious zeal felt or exhibited by the swordsmen of Islam before and after the "infidels" who resisted "were sent to hell", the Brahmans massacred or molested or expelled, idols desecrated, temples demolished, and mosques raised in their stead. The prophet of Islam appears in a dream and bids a sultān to start on the "holy expedition", leaving no doubt that the "victory of religion" was assured. Amīr Khusrū was very eloquent about the transformation that was taking place. When the hordes of Alāu'd-Dīn Khaljī sacked the temple of Somnath, he exulted, "The sword of Islām purified the land as the Sun purfies the earth." His enthusiasm broke all bounds when the same hordes swept over South India: "The tongue of the sword of the Khalifa of the time, which is the tongue of the flame of Islām, has imparted light to the entire darkness of Hindustān by the illumination of its guidance...and several capitals of the gods of the Hindus in which Satanism had prevailed since the time of Jinns, have been demolished. All these impurities of infidelity have been cleansed by the Sultān's destruction of idol-temples, beginning with his first expedition to Deogīr, so that the flames of the light of the law illumine all these unholy countries... Allah be praised !" One wonders whether this poet of Islam and a sūfī luminary is being honoured or slandered when he is presented in our own times as the pioneer of Secularism. Or, perhaps, Secularism in India has a meaning deeper than that we find in the dictionaries or dissertations on political science. We may not be much mistaken if, seeing its studied exercise in blackening everything Hindu and whitewashing everything Islamic, we suspect that this Secularism is nothing more than the good old doctrine of Islam in disguise.

If our citations prove anything and prove it beyond a shadow of doubt, it is this that in doing what they did to Hindu temples the heroes of Islam were inspired by their religion and religion alone. They cannot be blamed if the plunder which occasionally preceded the destruction of temples was viewed by them as a well-deserved reward for doing service to Allah and his Last Prophet; they knew what the Qur'ān and the Sunnah had prescribed and promised in very clear language and, therefore, had a clean conscience. It is a different matter altogether that their religion provided a cover (or an *a posteriori* justification as Professor Mohammed Habib would like to put it) for some of the basest motives in human nature and attracted to its standard some of the worst hoodlums and gangsters and blood-thristy bandits that the world has known. The fact that these despicable characters have been made to masquerade as *Mujāhids* and *Ghāzīs* and *Shahīds* and Sultāns and Sufis by Muslim historians can hoodwink no one except those who either do not know the facts or have the same moral standards as those of Islam.

Our Marxist professors and other pandits of Secularism are very much mistaken when they discover or invent economic and/or political motives for explaining away the crimes committed by Islam. Either they have remained totally ignorant of what the Theology of Islam prescribes vis-a-vis the unbelievers, their women and children, their properties, their homelands, their religious teachers, and their places of worship; or their deep-seated animus against everything Hindu has pushed them into the camp of those who are out to destroy everything for which this country has been held in high esteem down the ages. We shall, give them the benefit of doubt and assume that their ignorance of the Theology of Islam rather than their anti-Hindu animus is the culprit. We proceed to present that Theology in the chapter that follows.

CHAPTER TWO

ISLAMIC THEOLOGY OF ICONOCLASM

The destruction of Hindu temples at the hands of Islamized invaders continued for more than eleven hundred years, from the middle of the seventh century to the end of the eighteenth.[1] It took place all over the cradle of Hindu culture, from Sinkiang in the North to Tamil Nadu in the South, and from Seistan in the West to Assam in the East.[2]

All along, the iconoclasts remained convinced that they were putting into practice the highest tenets of their religion. They also saw to it that a record was kept of what they prized as a pious performance. The language of the record speaks for itself. It leaves no doubt that they took immense pride in doing what they did.

It is inconceivable that a constant and consistent behaviour pattern, witnessed for a long time and over a vast area, can be explained except in terms of a settled system of belief which leaves no scope for second thoughts. Looking at the very large number of temples, big and small, destroyed or desecrated or converted into Muslim monuments, economic or political explanations can be only a futile, if not a fraudulent, exercise. The explanations are not even plausible.

In fact, it is not at all difficult to locate the system of belief which inspired the behaviour pattern. We have only to turn to the scriptures of Islam—the Qur'ān and the Sunnah of the Prophet—and we run straight into what we are looking for. The principles which were practised, and the pious precedents which were followed by the subsequent swordsmen of Islam are, all of them, there.

The scriptures of Islam do not merely record what its Allah ordained and its prophet did in the past; they also prescribe that what is recorded should be imitated by the faithful in the future, till the end of time. That is why the swordsmen of Islam who functioned in times much later than that of the Qur'ān and the Sunnah, did what they did. It is in the very nature of scriptures, as we shall see, that they make permanent what can otherwise be dated and dismissed as temporary aberrations.

Those scriptures are still being taught in hundreds of *maktabs* and

---

[1]We are leaving for the time being the destruction that took place in Muslim princely states under British rule as also that which has continued since 1947 in Pakistan, Bangladesh and Kashmir.

[2]We are leaving for the time being the destruction which took place and is taking place in Indonesia and Malaysia.

madrasas spread over the length and breath of India, Pakistan and Bangladesh. Missionaries of Islam that are turned out by these institutions, year after year, are never told by their teachers that the prescriptions regarding other people's places of worship stand abrogated or are out of date. At the same time, the swordsmen who destroyed innumerable temples and monasteries all over the vast cradle of Hindu culture, retain their halos as the heroes of Islam. That alone can explain why Hindu temples become the first targets of attack whenever Muslim mobs are incited against India by the mullas in Pakistan, Bangladesh and Kashmir.

It is, therefore, worthwhile to clarify what the word "scripture" stands for, before we take up the scripures of Islam. The language of Christianity and Islam in the modern media has confused the language of religion, all along the line. Even scholars do not seem to know or care to clarify that scripures as such are specific to the prophetic or revealed religions such as Judaism, Christianity and Islam, and that they remain unknown to the pagan[3] spiritual traditions such as that of the Hindus, the Chinese, the ancient Iranians, and the pre-Christian Greeks, Romans, Germans, Slavs, Scandinavians, Celts, etc.

The confusion has been further confounded by what passes for Secularism in this country. Most of our scribes in the mass media are either equally ignorant of all religions or equally indifferent to them. But they insist, with considerable vehemence, that all religions say the same things. Politicians in power are much worse. As they preside over the birthday functions or festivals related to Śrī Rāma, Śrī Krishṇa, Bhagavān Mahāvīra, Bhagavān Buddha and Guru Nānak on the one hand, and Jesus Christ and Prophet Muhammad on the other, they harangue the audience to follow the teachings in each case. It never occurs to them that Christianity and Islam have nothing in common with the Hindu spiritual traditions and that the followers of the former have tried and are trying their utmost to wipe out the latter.[4]

MEANING OF SCRIPTURE

Etymologically, the wrod "scripture" is derived from the Latin "*scribere*", to write. In the lexicons of the revealed religions, however, the word does not refer to writing down of human speech or verbalizing

---

[3]The *Chambers 20th Century Dictionary* defines a pagan as "a heathen, one who is not a Christian, Jew, or Muslim..."

[4]The subject has been discussed in detail by Dr. Harsh Narain in his study, *Myths of Composite Culture and Equality of Religions*, published by Voice of India, New Delhi, 1991.

of human thought or recording of terrestrial events. Instead, it stands for the "Word of God" written in "the Book".

The word of God, in its turn, does not come to any and every one who seeks it, howsoever devoutly. Instead, it is "revealed" to some highly privileged persons known as "prophets". Everyone else has to learn it second-hand, and accept it as authentic even when it runs counter to one's experience, or reason, or moral sense, or all of them taken together. No one else can have direct knowledge of it or aspire to enter into the consciousness to which it was revealed, as in the case of pagan spiritual traditions which entitle every seeker to attain the consciousness of their greatest saints and sages and know God directly and first-hand. Belief in the word of God as spoken by *the* Prophet and as written in *the* Book is, therefore, all that is needed for qualifying as one of the faithful. At the same time, mental belief and not moral behaviour is the criterion for judging a person's character.

Nor do the prophets take birth among any or every people. Etymologically, the word "prophet" is derived from the Greek "*phanai*", to speak, which is a cognate of the Sanskrit "*bhaṇa*". In the lexicons of the revealed religions, however, the prophet is no ordinary spokesman. Instead, he is the "spokesman of deity."[5] And he is "sent" only to the "Chosen People" with whom God intends to enter into a "Covenant".

So far there have been only three chosen people—the Jews, the Christians, and the Muslims. According to the covenants which God has entered into with them, each of them has been promised world-dominion and untold amounts of unearned wealth in exchange for making God known to all those who worship "other gods" and thus deny God's "Unity" and "Unique Majesty".

RISE OF THEOLOGY

In due course, as the word of God is studied, systematized and interpreted, it gives birth to a supplementary discipline named Theology. Etymologically, the word "theology" is a compound of two Greek words—"theos"[6] meaning "god", and "logos" meaning "word". But curiously enough, the ancient Greeks from whose language the compound has been constructed were unaware of the very notion of word of God. Theology was formulated and used for the first time by the Founding Fathers of the Christian Church for presenting their peculiar

---

[5]See the *Chambers 20th Century Dictionary* for the Meaning of Prophet.
[6]It is a cognate of the Sanskrit "*deva*".

creed to pagans in the Roman Empire. It had nothing whatsoever to do with any Greek religion or philosophy, of which there were quite a few before they were destroyed or subverted by Christianity. Islamic scholarship which flourished in the wake of the Prophet, fashioned another theology, more or less on the same pattern, a few hundred years later.

Theology is a large and complex subject. What concerns us here is some specific features which characterise it. One of those features is that the life-style of the Prophet and his companions/apostles is proclaimed as the "divine pattern of human conduct" which should be copied by everyone, everywhere, in order to qualify for salvation or paradise. According to another, the doings of the chosen people as they wage wars, conquer countries, and convert or kill other people, are to be seen as the unfoldment of a "divine plan in human history".

What is most significant, however, is that theology notices and notifies three neat and sharp divisions. Firstly, it divides human history into two periods—an "age of ignorance" preceding the appearance of *the* Prophet, and an "age of illumination" following that event. Secondly, it bifurcates the human family into two factions—the "believers" who accept *the* Prophet as the one and only "mediator" between God and human beings, and the "unbelievers" who have either not heard of *the* Prophet at all or find him unacceptable for whatever reason. Thirdly, it breaks up the inhabited world into two camps—the lands ruled by the believers, and the lands where the unbelievers live.

Proceeding further, theology pronounces a permanent war, hailed as "holy", between the three sets of divisions. Religions and cultures which preceded in the age of ignorance have to go and yield place to the religion and culture of the age of illumination. Next, the believers must strive, ceaselessly and by every means at their disposal, to convert the unbelievers to the new creed. Finally, the lands of the believers must be made into launching pads for missions as well as military expeditions to be sent to the lands of the unbelievers, so that the latter are conquered and turned into lands of the believers.

Naturally, the places where the unbelievers worship and the institutions which sustain that worship, become the first and foremost targets of holy wars. The idols[7] of the unbelievers' Gods are at least mutilated, if they cannot be smashed to pieces. The temples where those Gods are worshipped are at least desecrated, if they cannot be destroyed. The schools and monasteries where the unbelievers learn their religion are

[7]The word "idol" is derived from the Greek "*idein*", to see, which is a cognate of the Sanskrit "*vid*", to perceive.

at least plundred, if they cannot be razed to the ground. The saints, sages and scholars who guide the unbelievers are at least humiliated, driven out and deprived of livelihood, if they cannot be killed outright. The literature which enshrines the unbelievers' religion and culture is scattered to the winds, or burnt on the spot, or used as fuel in the homes of the believers. And so on, the war on the religion and culture of the unbelievers is total and unrelenting.

These operations are expected to help the unbelievers lose faith in their own Gods and acqire an awe for the God of the conqueror. The God of the conqueror stands glorified when new places of worship are raised on the sites of the old, preferably with the debris of those that have been deliberately demolished. And that God is fully vindicated when the believers tread under foot the idols of the unbelievers' Gods or their pieces, as they walk towards the new places of worship for offering prayers.

Finally, theology enjoins that the holy wars and all that they mean should be recorded meticulously and in lustrous language. These records testify to the unfoldment of the divine plan in human history in the past, and inspire future generations of believers to unfold it further. We have three extensive versions of this unfoldment or the triumph of the "true faith" over "false belief"—the Judaic, the Christian, and the Islamic. All of them glorify the "great heroes" who waged holy wars and heaped defeats and humiliations on the "infidels". The "rich rewards" which God bestowed on the believers for fulfilling their part of the covenant are also described at length. And succeeding generations of believers have, no doubt, felt inspired to follow in the footsteps of their "illustrious forefathers".

ROLE OF THEOLOGY

Apart from providing the right perceptions, inspiring pious performances, and establishing illustrious precedents, theology serves another and, psychologically, a very useful purpose. It prepares the believers for feeling the "glow of faith" as they read or listen to the unfoldment of the divine plan in human history. The accounts are spiritually satisfying—how every trace of the religion and culture of the age of ignorance was wiped out, to start with, in the Prophet's own land of birth; how one land after another was invaded and laid waste without any provocation on the part of the victims of aggression; how innocent and defenceless people were massacred in cold blood and with a clean conscience; how the defeated unbelievers were converted to the true faith by means of overwhelming force; how large numbers of noncombatant men, women and children were captured and sold into slavery and concubinage; how native populations were reduced to the status of non-citizens, drawing water and hewing wood for the conqueror, and groaning under the weight of discriminatory levies and back-breaking disabilities; how great creations of graphic arts were mutilated or broken to pieces or trampled under foot; how edifices of exquisite beauty, embodying skills accumulated over ages, were pulled down and levelled with the ground; how whole libraries containing priceless works of science and literature, were burnt down; how saints and sages and scholars who had given no offence and meant no harm, were humiliated or manhandled or killed; how vast properties, moveable and immovable, were misappropriated. And so on, the record is invariably crowded with dark crimes and fiendish cruelty. It is only the believers who find it fulfilling. For persons with normal moral sensibilities, it is a nightmare. The only point which goes in its favour is that it provides the best commentary on the doctrines of the creed concerned.

Looking at the character of the God of revealed religions, the quality of his word, the life-style of his prophets, and the course of his divine plan in human history, one wonders whether the revealed religions do not reveal an Orwellian world abounding in marvels of double-think and double-speak. Here one meets the Devil masquerading as God, and gangsters strutting around as prophets. Here one discovers that the scripture does not inspire spiritual seeking or moral discipline but, on the contrary, encourages the basest in human nature to run riot without any restraint. All in all, theology stands out as another name for Demonology, and the revealed religions reveal themselves as no more than totalitarian ideologies of aggression, of imperialism, of enslavement, terror, and genocide. They turn out to be older versions of what we have known as Communism and Nazism in our own times. A Secularism which puts them on par with the spiritual traditions of Hinduism is not only foolish but also mischievous. It misses the very meaning of religion, and shelters gangsterism.

THEOLOGY OF ISLAM

Islam uses the Arabic language instead of Hebrew or Greek, but says the same things as the older revealed religions. Its only point of departure is that it abrogates the earlier revelations, and subordinates the earlier prophets to the "latest and the last".

Islam has hijacked Allāh from the pantheon of the pre-Islamic

Arabs and turned him into a "jealous God" who tolerates no "other gods". Allāh of Islam is no more than a reincarntion of Jehovah, the Judaic and the Christian God in the Bible.

The prophet of Islam, Muhammad, moulds himself, consciously and progressively, in the image of Moses. In fact, his very name, *Nabī*, has been taken from the Hebrew lexicon.

Allāh now speaks only through the mouth of Muhammad. That is the Qur'ān, or the Book *(Kitāb)*. Here also the word of God is borrowed, by and large, from the Bible. The only difference is that the Qur'ān lacks the literary merit and narrative coherence of the earlier scripture. It is a loose bundle of vehement utterances, without any chronological or thematic order, and has to be understood with the help of laborious, very often ludicrous, commentaries.

Again, Allāh acts in the life-style of Muhammad. That is the Sunnah of the Prophet. This divine pattern of human conduct knows all the answers. No pious Muslim has to use his own mental faculties or devise his own individual course of action. It is all laid down for him, from birth to death, and even beyond. As the theologians of Islam say, Muslims should not use their *aql* (reason), all they need is *naql* (imitation of the Prophet).

The covenant, *Miṣāq*, into which Allāh enters with the newly chosen people, the *Ummatu Muhammadī*, commands them to worship him alone and convert or kill or enslave those who worship "other gods". Allāh's earlier covenants with the Jews or the *Ummatu Ibrāhīmī* and the Christians or the *Ummatu Īsā*, stand cancelled. Now onwards, Muslims alone are entitled to rule over the world and appropriate its wealth. There is a slight "improvement" also in the new covenant. Plunder of the infidels' properties, particularly their women and children, was not permitted to the earlier chosen people, while it has been prescribed as obligatory for the *Ummatu Muhammadī*.

The doings of the *Ummatu Muhammadī* in Arabia and many other lands manifest the divine plan in human history. The annals of Islam, the *Twārīkh*, which are an integral part of its theology, have been penned by some of its most pious scholars.

The theology of Islam, *Kalām*, deals with the same old divisions of human history, the human family, and the inhabited world. The period before Muhammad started receiving revelations and proclaimed his prophethood is denounced as *Jāhilīya*, the age of ignorance; the period succeeding that event is the age of *Ilm*, enlightenment. Those who recite the *Kalima* or confession of faith—*Lā Ilāha Illa'llāhū, Maham-*

madūn Rasūl'llāh (there is no god but Allāh and Muhammad is *the* Prophet)[8]—are *Mu'mins*, the believers; those who do not, are *Kāfirs*, the unbelievers. The lands ruled by the *Mu'mins* are *Dār al-Islām*, abodes of peace, while those where the *Kāfirs* live are *Dār al-Harb*, abodes of war, where the *Mu'mins* should ply their swords. It sounds logical that in popular Muslim parlance a *Kāfir* is often called a *Harbī*, that is, one who deserves treatment of the sword.

Finally, Islam enjoins a permanent war, *Jihād*, by the *Mu'mins* and against the *Kāfirs*. A *Mu'min* becomes a *Mujāhid* when he participates in *Jihād*. A *Mujāhid* becomes a *Ghāzī* when he slaughters the *Kāfirs* with his own hands, and a *Shahīd* if he gets killed in the conflict. The highest honour in this hierarchy goes to the *Shahīd*. He does not have to wait for the Day of Judgement for entering *Jannat* (paradise) as is the case for mere *Mu'mins* and *Mujāhids* and *Ghāzīs*; he travels straight away to the embraces of the *Hūriyas*, the dark-eyed and eternally youthful maidens promised to all Muslims by their Allah. We need not give the details which we have already presented elsewhere, in principle as well as in practice.[9] Suffice it to say that it is an extremely bloody affair, entailing continued wars of conquest, massacres, mass conversions by force, widespread plunder, enslavement of prisoner taken in war, collection of booty including noncombatant men and women and children, subjugation of native populations, and the rest. What concerns us here is that *Jihād* is centred round iconoclasm. In fact, the need for *Jihād* arises only because the *Kāfirs* worship their own Gods instead of Muhammad's Allāh. *Jihād*, therefore, remains incomplete till all places where those Gods are worshipped get levelled with the ground, and all saints and priests who spread and sustain *Kufr* are converted or killed.

Confining ourselves to India, "The Mohammedan conquest of India is probably the bloodiest story in history," according to Will Durant, the famous student of civilizations. He finds it "a discouraging tale, for its evident moral is that civilization is a precious thing whose delicate complex of order and liberty, culture and peace may at any time be overthrown by barbarians..."[10] But the pious Muslims read or

---

[8]The first part of the *Kalima* is often translated as "there is no god but God," which is not only misconceived but positively mischievous. Allāh of the Qur'ān never claims to be the God of mankind; he prides in being the God of Muslims alone. The correct translation should be "there is no god but Allah."

[9]*The Calcutta Quran Petition By Chandmal Chopra*, with two prefaces by Sita Ram Goel, second the enlarged edition, New Delhi, 1987, pp. 35–37.

[10]Will Durant, *The Story of Civilization*. Vol. I, *Our Oriental Heritage*, New York, 1972, p. 459.

listen to this story with immense satisfaction. They go into raptures as their heroes invade Sind and Hind, massacre the "accursed *Kāfirs*" without remorse, capture and sell into slavery large numbers of Hindu men and women and children, kill or heap humiliations on Hindu saints and scholars, desecrate or destroy idols of Hindu Gods and Goddesses, pull down Hindu temples or convert them into *masjids* and *madrasas*, reduce the Hindus to non-citizens in their own homeland, and misappropriate all properties, moveable and immovable. And they get furious when they find the Hindus failing to admire Muhammad bin Qāsim, Mahmūd of Ghazni, Muhammad Ghūrī, Shamsu'd-Dīn Iltutmish, Ghiyāsu'd-Dīn Balban, 'Alāu'd-Dīn Khaljī, Muhammad and Fīrūz Shāh Tughalaq, Sikandar Lodī, Bābur, Aurangzeb, and Ahmad Shāh Abdālī, to cite only the most notable among Muslim heroes in the history of India. The theology of Islam has thus performed to perfection the function it is intended to perform, even though the forefathers of an overwhelming majority of Muslims in India were victims of this theology.

In our specific context, namely, the destruction of Hindu temples, it should be more than sufficient if we merely cite what the Qur'ān says, in verse after verse and chapter after chapter, vis-a-vis the *mushriks* (polytheists) and the *aṣnām* (idols) they worship. Allāh of Islam leaves no one in doubt that he sanctions the destruction of "false gods" and the places where they receive homage. So is the case with the Sunnah of the Prophet. We have only to list the instances of iconoclasm which Muhammad undertook himself or ordered in his own lifetime, and we have more than suffcient pious precedents which the faithful are expected to follow. Anyone who says that the Qur'ān and the Sunnah do not enjoin the destruction of other people's places of worship has either not read the documents, or has failed to grasp the message, or is practising deliberate deception. No amount of apologetics can cover up or explain away the principle and the practice.

Chapter Three

ICONOCLASM IN THE QUR'ĀN

The verses (*āyats*) which deal with idolatry and idolaters lie scattered in all chapters (*Sūras*) of the Qur'ān; taken together they constitute the largest number, particularly in the Meccan Sūras, as compared to those devoted to other subjects. Many a time, the verses occur in the stories of prophets who came before Muhammad. But it is more than obvious that they are addressed to the pagan contempories of the Prophet. We have collected and collated them under several sections as the theme develops, stage by stage, till it reaches its climax, that is, Allāh's threat to destroy all peoples and human settlements where gods other than him are honoured.

The "other gods" mean idols, most of the time; this is clear by the word *ṣanam* (pl. *aṣnām*) which stands for carved statues, and *wathan* (pl. *awthān*) which stands for simple stones, trimmed or untrimmed. Sometimes the "other gods" are the Stars, the Sun and the Moon as well; worship of these heavenly bodies was prevalent in pagan Arabia. But the description which we find most frequent in the Qur'ān is "partners ascribed to Allāh". The technical term used for this ascription is *shirk* which literally means "mixing" or "associating". The idolaters are consequently called *mushriks*, which term has acquired a terrible stink in Islamic parlance. Witnessing the tantrums which Allāh throws constantly about "partners ascribed to him", we are left with a strong impression that the pagans had never neglected Allāh; they only preferred to worship him surrounded by his numerous companions who were his own Aspects, Names and Forms.[1]

Surveying the scene in pagan Arabia, Allāh of the Qur'ān notices with great anger as well as anguish that, though most of them worship Allāh, they always ascribe partners to him. What is worse, they worship female deities such as Al-Lāt, Al-Manāt and Al-'Uzzā, calling them daughters of Allāh.[2] They do not know that Allāh never had a consort

---

[1] Some scholars say that Muhammad used the term "partners" because he was a businessmen. This sounds to be true. Allāh of the Qur'ān does look like a racketeer out to consolidate a monopoly over worship which humans offer to the Divine.

[2] A translator of the Qur'ān oberves in a footnote that these Arab Goddesses were like Lakshmī and Sarasvatī of the Hindus (*Qur'ān Majīd* translated into Hindi by Muhammad Fārūq Khān, Rampur (U.P.), sixth reprint, 1976, p. 242). Hindus can accept the observation as a complement, though the translator frowns upon their Goddesses as "mere names without reference to any existence". In any case, it establishes kinship between Hindus and the Arab pagans. Hindu Gods and Godesses have invited the some invectives and physical onslaughts from the Islamic invaders and their remanants as the Arab Gods and Godesses did from the Prophet and his flock.

and, therfore, no sons or daughters. They are also unfair to Allāh when they burden him with daughters, while they prefer sons for themselves.[3] Allāh informs the idolaters that these female deities are "mere names" invented by their forefathers and repeated by them, and that the worship of other divinities, male or female, has received "no warrant", that is, no scriptural sanction. The "idolaters" are also accused of dividing their offerings between Allāh and the partners ascribed to him. But no offerings ever reach Allāh because the partners grab his portion as well as their own. And their worship in the Ka'ba is "naught but whistling and handclapping."[4] It seems that, like pagans everywhere and at all times, the pagans of Arabia also worshipped their Gods with song and dance.

Allāh also complains that the pagans pray to Allāh only when they are in trouble, but turn to "other gods" as soon as they are out of it. If asked why they do not worship Allāh alone and always, they say that they follow "the way of their forefathers"; they do not know that their forefathers wer "unintelligent" and had received "no guidance". They also forget that it is Allāh who has created them and provides for them. On the contrary, they have invented lies in support of which they come out with no proof. And they persist in their error even when a Book has been sent to them. They have chosen mere "slaves" as their protectors instead of the "master", that is, Allāh without realizing that slaves control nothing and can protect no one. Nor do they grasp the "simple truth" that if there were gods beside Allāh, "both heaven and earth would have got disordered". The most unkindest cut of all, however, is that they invite Muhammad to disbelive in Allāh and turn to their gods. But Muhammad has not only no knowledge of their gods, he has also received proof to the contrary. It is the same proof which the earlier prophets had received. The idolaters thus compound their error by trying to drag Allāh's prophet down to their own degenerate level.[5]

Turning to Muhammad, Allāh issues a stern command: "Say: O mankind ! If you are in doubt about my religion then (know) that I worship not what you worship instead of Allāh, but I worship Allāh who causeth you to die, and I have been commanded to be of the believers...[6] There is no compulsion in religion. The right direction is henceforth distinct from error, and he who rejects false deities and be-

[3] Allāh of the Qur'ān, like Jehovah of the Bible, has great contempt for females. See Qur'ān, 16.57;37.149–53; 43.16-19; 52.39; 53.21-22,27; 65.1-7.

[4] Qur'ān, 12.106; 4.117; 6.101-102; 59.19-23; 6.137; 8.35.

[5] Ibid., 3.93; 2.170; 30.40; 18.15; 4.153; 18.102; 21.22; 40.42; 40.66.

[6] Ibid., 10.40.

lieves in Allāh alone has grasped a firm handhold which will never break. Allāh is Hearer, Knower.'[7]

Coming to the "other gods", the cause of the whole quarrel, Allāh makes it quite clear that he himself has not appointed them, nor authorised their worship. The prophets and scriptures sent by him earlier can be consulted on the subject. He challenges the "idolaters" to produce proof to the contrary, if they have any. On the other hand, he has sent a scripture to Muhammad confirming the earlier prophets, and prohibiting the pagan practices in very clear words. The other gods "possess not an atom's weight either in heaven or on earth, nor have they any share in either". They do not "own so much as the white spot on a date-stone".[8]

Allāh waxes eloquent about his own creation, which includes everything in the Cosmos; the Qur'ān is crowded with verses in which its author revels in unbounded self-adultation. The exercise over, he challenges the "idolaters" to produce evidence that "their gods" have ever created anything. The truth, he says, is that they cannot create but are themselves created. They are dead, not living. If the "idolaters" want to know the worth of "their gods", they should call them (the gods) and wait for an answer; they will wait in vain. For, "the gods" have no ears with which they may hear, and no eyes with which they may see. Also, they have no feet with which they may walk, and no hands with which they may hold anything. They are helpless, and dwell in darkness.[9]

Being deaf, dumb, blind and without limbs, the "other gods" can neither help, nor hurt. If a fly snatches away something from them, they do not have the strength to get it back. They are as frail and fragile as a spider's web. They cannot come to the rescue of those whom Allāh wants to hurt. Those who hope to be helped by the "other gods" on the Last Day, are in for great disappointment; they (the gods) have not been given any power of intercression on anyone's behalf. They can lead their devotees only to doom because they are "Satan's handiworks" like "strong drink and games of chance."[10]

Allāh confides to Muhammad that he will set the devils to sow confusion in the camp of idolatry. The "other gods" will turn against

---

[7] Ibid., 2.256. The first line of this verse is often cited by apologists of Islam in support of their proposition that Islam stands for tolerance in matters of belief. The complete verse, however, says quite clearly that the unbelievers have no business to persist in error after the right guidance has come. All commentators on the Qur'ān proclaim, in unmistakable language, that this verse authorises Muslims to wipe out all other religions.

[8] Ibid., 48.47; 21.24-25; 34.22; 35.13.

[9] Ibid., 31.11; 25.3; 16.17; 16.21; 7.194-194; 13.16.

[10] Ibid., 25.55; 21.43; 29.40; 17.56; 36.23; 19.15; 43.86; 5.90.

their worshippers, and vice versa. The doors of hell will be opened and the "idolaters" will be thrown into blazing fire. It is then that they (the idolaters) will admit that they were wrong-doers and bewail that "their gods" had failed them. They will wish to have another life on earth, so that they may be among the believers. But it will be too late. "Bound in chains, they will be dragged through boiling waters." No mediator will come forward to mediate for them.[11]

Next, Allāh recites the record of earlier prophets and wise men vis-a-vis the idols and idolaters. We will relate it chronologically.

Abraham chided his father Ezra and his people for being idolaters. He also rejected the worship of the Stars, the Moon and the Sun, all of which he saw setting after rising. His people argued with him in favour of the ancestral way of worship. He asked them to produce scriptural proof in defence of their gods. At the same time, he sought forgiveness from Allāh for his father. He harangued his father not to worship "those who neither hear, nor see, nor are helpful in any way." His father rejected the advice and threatened to stone him. Abraham now decided to demonstrate the worthlessness of the "other gods". He sneaked into a place of worship when his people were away and smashed all the idols to pieces except the biggest one among them. The people, when they came back and saw the scene, made enquiries. Some young men who had seen Abraham doing the deed reported the matter to them. So Abraham was questioned. He pointed an accusing finger at the big idol and said that the big one had smashed the smaller ones, and that the truth could be found out by questioning the pieces. His people said that idols were not known to speak. He shouted back, "Why then do you worship them? Fie on you and what you worship !" They got angry and tried to burn him alive. But Allāh cooled the fire and saved him. He told his people that it was not he but they and "their gods" who were "fuel for hell-fire", where they will be tormented for ever. Then he separated himself from his people and proclaimed, "There has arisen between us and you hostility and hatred for ever until you believe in Allāh." Before he left, he informed his father, "I have sought forgiveness for you, though I know nothing for you from Allāh." His devotion was rewarded by Allāh with a son, Issac, and a grandson, Jacob.[12]

Moses found his people adoring the golden calf soon after he brought them out of Egypt. He ordered them to slaughter with their own hands those among them who had gone astray. It was done. Moses

[11] Ibid., 19.82-83; 16.86; 26.19-102; 40.74; 74.48.
[12] Ibid., 6.75-82; 14.41; 19.42; 21.57-69, 98-100; 26 86; 60.4; 26.77.

also cursed Sāmirī, the man who had connived at the worship of the golden calf, so that Sāmirī became "a leper in this life and fuel for hell-fire in the next". Moses burnt the golden calf and "scattered the ashes on the sea."[13]

Solomon was informed by his pet hooper that the people of Saba' (Sheba of the Bible) were ruled by a woman and worshipped the Sun instead of Allāh. He wrote to the Queen of Saba' demanding that she and her people should come to the true faith. The Queen took fright and consulted her chieftains who went in a delegation to Solomon with rich presents. The king spurned the presents and demanded that the Queen be present in his court to settle the matter. The Queen had no choice. She went to Jerusalem, saw Solomon's power, and accepted that there was "no god beside Allāh."[14]

Elijah warned his people not to worship Ba'al. They disregarded his advice and will face the doom on the Day of Judgment. Luqmān advised his son not to be an idolater, and to serve his parents. But if anyone's parents pressed their son to ascribe partners to Allāh, they were to be disobeyed. Ties of faith stood above ties of kinship. Coming down the road of time, seven young men in Palestine took refuge inside a cave and went to sleep when they saw their people degenerating into idolatry. They slept for three hundred years and thought it only a day when they were awakened by Allāh. One of them went out to find food and discovered that the Roman Empire was rid of idolatry and was worshiping Allāh alone. The people in the town also learnt about the true believers in the cave and hailed them as followers of Jesus Christ. A mosque was erected over their graves when the seven faithful died after some time.[15]

Some of these stories are repeated several times and spread over several Sūras. Allāh tells them again and again for the benefit of the "idolaters" of Arabia. He exhorts them to follow the path of Abraham, Moses, Solomon, Elijah, Luqmān and the seven young men; otherwise they were bound to become "fuel for hell-fire". Had there been any other gods, they themselves would have tried to "reach the throne and usurp Allāh's authority; there would have been disorder in heaven as well as on earth."[16] If the "idolaters" fail to repent, Allāh threaterns to "cast terror in their hearts"; he tells them clear and loud that "their

[13] Ibid, 2.54; 29.96-97.
[14] Ibid., 27.22-24.
[15] Ibid, 37.123-128; 31.13-15; 18.9-21.
[16] Ibid., 3.95; 17.39; 42; 21.22; 3.151; 4.41; 14.30; 18.52; 39.16; 21.39.

abode will be hell-fire". He can never forgive idolatry which is the greatest crime. They will find no escape from the torments in hell, "which is their journey's end". There will be "an awning of fire above them, and a floor of fire underneath; they will not be able to drive it away from their faces, nor from their backs". We are leaving out the blood-curdling accounts, which abound in the Qur'ān, about what the fire will do to the "idolaters", again and again, and for ever and ever.[17]

Finally, Allāh bares his fangs and comes out in his true colours. "And how many generations," he thunders, "We destroyed before them!...Had they any place of refuge? ...and they cried out when it was no longer time for escape... Not one of them but denied the messenger, therefore My doom was justified... We seized them unawares and lo ! they were dumb-founded. So of the people who did wrong the last remnant was cut off... And the heavens and the earth wept not for them, nor were they reprieved... How many townships have we destroyed! As a raid by night, or while they slept at noon, Our terror came upon them... Have they not travelled in the land and seen the nature of the consequences for those who were before them, and they were mightier than these in power? Say (unto them, O Muhammad): Travel in the land and see the nature of the sequel for the guilty! ...And when We would destroy a township, We send commandments to its folk who live at ease, and afterwards they commit abomination therein, and so the word (of doom) hath effect for it, and we annihilate it with complete annihilation...There is not a township but we shall destroy it ere the Day of Resurrection and punish it with dire punishment... And we verily have destroyed townships round about you... Allāh struck at the foundations of their buildings, and then the roof fell down upon them from above them, and the doom came upon them whence they knew not... Are they who plan ill-deeds then secure that Allāh will not cause the earth to swallow them? ...Or that He will not seize them in their going to and fro so that there be no escape for them? ...So think not that Allāh will fail to keep His promise to His messenger. Lo! Allāh is Mighty, Able to Requite."[18]

Lest the idolaters entertain the illusion that Allāh is bragging and does not mean business, he names the tribes and towns he destroyed in olden times. Nūh had warned his people repeatedly against idolartry.

---

[17] For detailed description of the torment see Ibid., 2.24; 4.56; 7.42; 10.4; 14.16-17; 17.97; 18.19;20.74; 22.19-22; 35.36-37; 44.44, 50; 69.30-36.

[18] Ibid, 50,36; 38.3.14; 6.44-45; 44.29; 7.4; 35.44; 27.69; 17.16,58; 46.27; 16.26,45,46; 14.47. "Able to Requite is a very mild translation of the Arabic "*Azīz al-Intiqām*", which means "Lover of Vengeance".

But they refused to renounce the "gods of their forefathers". Allāh sent heavy rains, waters rose on all sides, and they were drowned.[19] Hūd taught his people in Ād not to worship any gods besides Allāh. They too were not prepared to give up the "gods of their forefathers". Allāh sent violent storms which raged for seven nights and eight days, and they were swept away.[20] Sālih was sent as a prophet to his people in Thamūd. He invited them to worship Allāh alone and throw away their idols. They did not listen to him. Instead, they hamstrung his camel. Allāh caused an earthquake along with a great thunderclap in the sky, which turned their town upside down and they were buried in the debris.[21] Lūt lived in Sadūm when Allāh's angels arrived to punish the inhabitants for their sinfulness. The prophet advised them to repent and seek refuge in Allāh. They turned a deaf ear and threatened to throw him out. Allāh rained stones on them, and the town together with its people was totally destroyed.[22] Shua'ib invited the people of Madayan (Midian) to turn to Allāh. Their chiefs invited him to renounce Islam. Allāh's wrath caught up with them.[23] Mūsā and Hārūn were sent to Fir'ūn (Pharoah), and showed him many signs from Allāh. But Fir'ūn refused to become a believer, and threatened to imprison the prophets. He was drowned in the sea along with his army.[24] The "dwellers of Ar-Raas" and "folk of Tubba'" also denied the messengers whom Allāh had sent to them. They were wiped out.[25]

Hindus will do well to read and interpret the Qur'ān with the help of orthodox commentaries written by renowned *imāms* of Islam, rather than rely on the motivated and mischievous summaries written by "Pandit" Sunderlal and Rahul Sankrityayana, or on the silly commentaries penned by Dr. Bhagwan Das and Acharya Vinoba Bhave in the spirit of *sarva-dharma-samabhāva.* Nothing can be more dangerous than a doctrine of terrorism which is either deliberately misrepresented or wilfully misunderstood.

---

[19] Ibid., 71.21-28. The story is repeated in several other chapters.

[20] Ibid., 6.65; 7.70; 11.58; 26.136-140; 54.18-21. The story is repeated in several other chapters.

[21] Ibid., 7.73-74; 11.62-65; 26.158-159; 54.23-31. The story is repeated in several other chapters.

[22] Ibid., 7.80-84; 11.77-83; 26.54-58. The name of the town, Sadūm (Sodom of the Bible) is not mentioned in the Qur'ān but is given by commentators. The stroy is repeated in several other chapters.

[23] Ibid., 7.85.93. The story is found in several other chapters.

[24] Ibid., 10.148–53; 26.18-29; 28.40-42. The story is found in many other chapters.

[25] Ibid., 50.10-14. These places have not been identified with certainty.

CHAPTER FOUR

ICONOCLASM IN THE SUNNAH

It is difficult to say at what stage of his life Muhammad became a convinced monotheist. The evidence available suggests that his evolution towards this creed was a slow process. Dealing with the years after his marriage to Khadījah and before he became a prophet, Margoliouth cites old Islamic sources and concludes that Muhammad was an idolater for quite some time. "The names of some of the children show that their parents when they named them were idolaters. Nor is there anything to indicate that Mohammed was at this time of a monotheistic or religious turn of mind. He with Khadijah performed some domestic rite in honour of one of the goddesses each night before retiring. At the wedding of his cousin, Abu Lahab's daughter, he is represented as clamouring for sport...He confessed to having at one time sacrified a grey sheep to Al-'Uzza—and probably did so more than once...A story which may be true shows us Mohammed with his stepson inviting the Meccan monotheist Zaid, son of 'Amr, to eat with them—of meat offered to idols: the old man refused..."[1]

Islamic hagiography, however, tells us that the Prophet was an uncompromising monotheist and a determined iconoclast from the moment he was conceived in the womb of his mother. "It is related that on the morning of conception the idols in all the inhabited quarters of the earth were overturned..."[2] Mightier events took place on the night of his birth. A lake dried up, a river overflowed and the palace of the Persian monarch "so trembled that fourteen of its pinnacles fell to the ground." More significantly "news arrived from Estakhan that the fire of the chief temple of Persia, which had burned for a thousand years, had become extinguished."[3] Nearer home, the Pagans in Mecca witnessed a scene which left them distressed. "Another event of the night of the nativity took place when the Qoraish were holding a festival in honour of one of their idols, in whose temple they had at that time assembled, and were engaged in eating and drinking. They found, however, that their god had fallen to the ground, and set him up again; but as he was, a short time afterwards, again found prostrate on his

[1] D.S. Margoliouth, *Mohammed and the Rise of Islam*, New Delhi Reprint, 1985, pp. 69-70.

[2] *The Rauzal-us-Safa, or Garden of Purity* by Muhhamad Khāvandshāh bin Mahmūd translated into English by E. Rehastek, Delhi Reprint, 1982, Vol. I, Part I, p. 85.

[3] Ibid., pp. 89–90.

face, the idolaters were much dismayed and erected him again. When they had done so the third time, a voice was heard from the cavity of the idol saying:

All the regions of the earth, in the east and west,
Respond to the nativity, whom its light strikes;
And idolatry decreases, and the hearts of all
The kings of the earth tremble with fear."[4]

As a baby, Muhammad was suckled by a desert woman, Ḥalīma. One day she came to Mecca to see the 'Ukāz fair, carrying Muhammad with her. An astrologer saw the baby and shouted, "Come here, O people of Hudayl, come here, O Arabs." People gathered round him, Ḥalīma among them. He pointed towards the baby and said, "He will slaughter people of your religion and smash your idols." Ḥalīma took fright and ran away with the baby.[5]

Muhammad was more than three years old when Ḥalīma took him to Mecca with the intention of returning him to his family. But the child got lost when they arrived in the city. Ḥalīma was searching frantically for him when she met an old man who heard her story and wanted to help. "The foolish man," says the biographer, "went to Hobal, and after praising him as is the fashion of idolaters, he continued: 'This woman of the Bani Sa'ad says that she lost Muhammad the son of A'bd-ul-Muttalib; restore him to her if it so pleaseth thee'... As soon as that misguided individual had pronounced these words Hobal fell prostrate on his face, and from the cavity of his statute the words were heard: 'What have I to do with Muhammad who will be the cause of our destruction? ...Tell the idolaters that he is the great sacrifice; that is to say, he will kill all, except those who will be so fortunate as to follow him.'"[6]

Muhammad was a young boy when he was invited by his uncles and aunts to join a celebration in honour of Buāna, a God to whom the Quraysh were much devoted. He was reluctant but yielded under pressure from the family. But when he came back, he was terribly frightened and looked depressed. His aunts asked what had happened to him. He said, "Whenever I went near an idol, I saw a man, white and tall, calling out to me, 'O Muhammad! get back, do not touch it.'"[7] He never joined a pagan celebration again.

---

[4] Ibid., p. 92.

[5] Translated from 'Alāma Abdullāh al-Ahmdī's Urdu version of *Tabqāt-i-ibn Sa'd,* Part I: *Akhbār an-Nabi,* Karachi, (n.d.), p. 233.

[6] *The Rauzat-us-Safa,* op. cit., Vol. I, pt. II, p. 115.

[7] Translated from the Urdu version of *Tabqāt-i-Ibn Sa'd,* Part I: *Akhbār an-Nabī,* Karachi, n.d., pp. 245–46.

Some time later, his people were sacrificing to Buāna. A voice came out of the idol's belly, "A strange thing has happened. We are being burnt in fire. Abeyance of *wahy* (revelation) has come to an end. A prophet has taken birth in Mecca. His name is Ahmad. He will migrate to Yathrib."[8]

His uncle, Abū Tālib, had taken Muhammad with a caravan going to Syria. The caravan halted near a monastery at Bostra where Bahira, a Christian monk, felt drawn towards Muhamad and made enquiries about him from the other Arabs. "When the people had finished eating," reports Ibn Ishāq, "and gone away Bahira got up and said to him, 'Boy, I ask you by al-Lāt and al-'Uzzā to answer my questions.' Now Bahira said this only because he had heard his people swearing by these gods. They allege that the apostle of God said to him, 'Do not ask me by al-Lāt and al-'Uzzā, for by Allah nothing is more hateful for me than these two gods.'"[9]

A similar event is reported to have happened in his youth when he was employed by Khadījah and travelled to Egypt with her merchandise. The caravan came across another Christian monk named Nasṭṭur who also fell for Mohammad. "Nasṭṭur...descended from the roof of his hermitage, and said to the apostle of Allah: 'I adjure thee by Lāt and U'zza to tell me what thy name is.' His holy and prophetic lordship replied : 'May thy mother be childless! Begone from me; for the Arabs have not uttered any words more disagreeable to me than thine.'"[10] At a latter stage in the same journey Muhammad had a dispute with a Jew on account of some business transaction. The Jew said; "I adjure you by Lāt and U'zza." Muhammad replied: "Whenever I pass by Lāt and U'zza, I turn away my face from them."[11]

Now, it is well-known that hagiography everywhere projects future events into the past. We have quoted from the hagiography of the Prophet not to decry it but to make the point that Islamic lore has always looked at Muhammad as a born iconoclast. This was not necessary because only his practices as a prophet provide the pious precedents. But hagiography hates to leave any loopholes, even if it has to invent events.

Hagiography yields place to history as we move into the period of Muhammad's prophethood. While initiating 'Alī b. Abū Tālib into Is-

---

[8] Ibid., p. 250. Idols can speak when it concerns prophets.

[9] Ibn Ishāq, *Sīrat Rasūl Allāh*, translated by A. Gillaume as *The Life of Muhammad*, OUP, Eighth Impression, Karachi, 1987, p. 80.

[10] *The Rauzat-us-Safa,* op. cit., p. 127.

[11] Ibid., p. 128.

lam, Muhammad said: "I call you to God, the One without associate, to worship him and to disavow al-Lāt and al-'Uzzā." 'Alī was surprised as he had never heard such a thing before, and offered to consult his father, Abū Tālib. But Muhammad told him, "If you do not accept Islam, then conceal the matter." Next morning, 'Alī came and requested Muhammad to initiate him. He had made up his mind after a night's reflection. Muhammad said to him, "Bear witness that there is no god but Allah alone without associate, and disavow al-Lāt and al-'Uzzā." 'Alī became a Muslim but "concealed his Islam and did not let it be seen."[12] Islam at this time was a secret society.

Ibn Hanbal cites another tradition from 'Ali about what the Prophet attempted while Islam was being kept concealed. 'Alī said: "I and the Prophet walked till we came to the Ka'ba. Then the Prophet of Allāh said to me, 'Sit down.' Then he stood on my shoulders and I arose. But when he saw that I could not support him, he came down, sat down and said, 'Stand on my shoulders.' Then I climbed on his shoulders and he stood up and it seemed to me as if I could have touched the sky, had I wished. Then I climbed on the roof of the Ka'ba on which there was an image of copper and iron. Then I began to loosen it at its right and left side, in front and behind until it was in my power. Then the Prophet of Allāh called to me: 'Throw it down.' Then I threw it down so that it broke into pieces like a bottle. I then climbed down from the Ka'ba and hurried away with the Prophet, till we hid ourselves in the houses for fear some one might meet us."[13] Shi'ah theologians have transferred this adventure to the time when the Prophet reached the Ka'ba after the conquest of Mecca.[14] But that is no more than a sectarian exercise. The language of the tradition connects the event to the time when Islam was still a secret society. Moreover, 'Alī is shown as a boy rather than a stalwart which he had become by the time Mecca was conquered.

Another incident relates to the time after Islam had come out into the open. It was reported to Hamzah, the Prophet's uncle, that Abū'l Ḥakam, a Meccan chief whom the Muslims called Abū Jāhl, had insulted Muhammad. Hamzah was still a pagan and, therfore, cared for kinship ties. He went to Muhammad who was sitting in the precincts of the Ka'ba, and said, "Thy uncle hast come to take vengeance on thy enemy." Muhammad asked him to leave alone the man "who has no

---

[12]Insert from Ibn Khallikān in Ibn Ishāq, op. cit., p. 115.

[13]*First Encyclopaedia of Islam 1931–36*, Leiden Reprint 1987, Vol. VII, p. 562.

[14]See *The Rauzat-us-Safa*, op. cit., Vol. II, pt. II, pp. 599–600. Also Saiyid Safdar Hosain, *The Early History of Islam*, Lucknow 1933, Delhi Reprint 1985, Vol. I, pp. 193–94.

uncle, neither father nor mother, no man of business, nor wazir," meaning himself. "But Hamzah swore by Lāt and U'zza saying, 'I have come only to aid and protect thee.'" The Prophet felt annoyed at his uncle's mention of the pagan Goddesses, and said, "I swear by that God who has sent me in truth, that if thou fightest long enough against infidels to be drowned in their blood, thou will only be removed further and further from the Lord of unity, until thou sayest, 'I bear witness that there is no god but Allah, and I testify that Muhammad is the apostle of Allah.'"[15]

On the whole, however, the situation in Mecca was unfavourable to the Prophet. The Pagans were in a strong position and he could not touch their idols or places of worship, howsoever keen he might have been to desecrate or destroy them. His attempt to invite another Abyssinian invasion of Mecca for taking over the Ka'ba and turning it into a place of monotheistic worship, was also a failure. The Christian king was very kind to the Muslims whom Muhammad had sent to his court. His doemstic situation, however, did not permit a foreign adventure. The Prophet's attempt to raise Tā'if against Mecca also ended in failure. He found himself utterly helpless against the pagan stronghold. He could only curse the "idolaters" and invoke Allāh's wrath against them.

It was in Medina that his followers started doing something concrete vis-a-vis the idols, after they had entered into a pact with him at al-'Aqaba for moving his headquarters to their city. Ibn Ishāq reports, "When they came to Medina they openly professed Islam there. Now some of the shykhs still kept to their old idolatry, among whom was 'Amr b. al-Jamūh...whose son Mu'ādh had been present at al-'Aqaba and done homage to the apostle there. 'Amr was one of the tribal nobles and leaders and had set up in his house a wooden idol called Manāt as the nobles used to do, making it a god to reverence and keeping it clean. When the young men of B. Salama...and his own son Mu'ādh adopted Islam with the other men who had been at al-'Aqaba they used to creep in at night to this idol of 'Amr's and carry it away and throw it on its face into a cesspit. When the morning came 'Amr cried, 'Woe to you! Who has been at our gods this night?' Then he went in search of the idol and when he found it he washed it and cleaned it and perfumed it saying, 'By God, if I knew who had done this I would treat him shamefully.' When night came and he was fast asleep they did the same again and he restored the idol in the morning...

[15] *The Rauzat-us-Safa*. op. cit., p. 179.

This happened several times..."[16]

The Prophet stayed at Qubā' in the course of his flight from Mecca. This was a place three miles outside Medina. A mosque was built here during the Prophet's stay. It was the first mosque in the history of Islam. The details of the site on which it was built are not available in the sources. But we are told something about the second and the major mosque built by the Prophet in Medina, soon after his arrival in that city. The site was a garden which he purchased. According to a tradition from Anas b. Mālik, "There were graves of the idolaters, dilapidated buildings and date trees [in the garden]. The Prophet gave the order and the graves of the idolaters were dug out, the dilapidated buildings levelled [with the ground], and the date trees cut down."[17] Most probably the site was a sacred grove and the buildings that stood there were places of pagan worship, neglected or abandoned due to the rising tide of monotheism in Medina. This much at least is certain that the Prophet showed contempt for the graves of the idoalters. In days to come, Muslims will show veneration for graves in which their own brothers in faith are buried. Cutting down of date trees was also a sacrilege according to pagan ethics.

'Alī found a Muslim at Qubā' stealing idols in the night and getting them burnt. Ibn Ishāq proceeds, "He used to say that in Qubā' there was an unmarried Muslim woman and he noticed that a man used to come to her in the middle of the night and knock on her door; she would come out and he would give her something. He felt very suspicious of him and asked her what was the meaning of this nightly performance as she was a Muslim woman without a husband. She told him that he was Sahl b. Hunayf b. Wāhib who knew that she was all alone and he used to break up the idols of his tribe at night and bring her the pieces to use as fuel..."[18]

The available sources provide no evidence of the Prophet or his followers in Medina desecrating or destroying any pagan shrines or breaking idols, during the many expeditions they mounted on tribal settlements, far and near. It is unlikely that the biographers of the Prophet or other Muslim annalists would have suppressed the facts on this score, for acts of iconoclasm were a matter of pride for them and an essential element in their glorification of Islam. Most propbably the

---

[16] Ibn Ishāq, op. cit., pp. 207.

[17] Translated from the Urdu version of *Sahīh Bukhārī Sharīf*, New Delhi, 1984, Vol. I, p. 240. See also the Urdu version of *Sunn Nasāī Sharīf*, New Delhi, 1986, Vol. I, p. 240, and *Tārīkh-i-Tabarī*, Vol. I, *Sīrat an-Nabī*, Karachi (n.d), p. 145.

[18] Ibn Ishaq, op. cit., pp. 227–28.

Muslims did not get proper opportunities for this, their favourite pastime, because most of the expeditions were surprise raids aimed at plunder, or assassination, or both. It is also probable that the Prophet did not want to show his hand before the right time and thus provoke more than normal resistance to his acts of aggression. Or, perhaps, it was the Prophet's strategy to break the morale of the Pagans by slaughter and rapine before he moved on to their places of worship. Whatever the reason, all available evidence suggests that the Prophet was busy throughout this period in amassing booty and ransom for financing his military machine, and recruiting desperados for the final assault on Mecca.

The Muslim army that finally moved on Mecca in the year AH 8 (AD 630) was a formidable force by Arabian standards of that time. Abbas b. Mirdās al-Sulamī, the Muslim, poet sang:

With us on the day Muhammad entered Mecca
Were a thousand marked men—the valley flowed with them.
They had helped the aspostle and been present at his battles,
Their marks on the day of battle being to the fore.
In a strait place their feet were firm.
They split the enemies' heads like colocynths.
Their hooves had travelled Najd beforehand
Till at last black Ḥijāz became subject to them.
God gave him the mastery of it.
The judgment of the sword and victorious fortune subdued it to us...[19]

Small wonder that Mecca surrendered without a fight. The pagan leader, Abū Sufyān, developed cold feet as soon as he saw the marshalled ranks, and went over to Islam. Very soon, he will be breaking the idols for which he had fought for long. "Abū Sufyān recited the following verses in which he excused himself for what had gone before:

By the life when I carried a banner
To give al-Lāt's cavalry the victory over Muhammad
I was like the one going astray in the darkness of the night,
But now I am led on the right track...[20]

The conquest of Mecca by Muhammad was the most significant event in the history of Islam. The success of the enterprise settled the character of Islam for all time to come. The lessons drawn from the

[19] Ibn Hishām's notes in Ibn Ishāq, op. cit., p. 775. "Marked men" means men carrying military colours or standards signifying various formations.

[20] Ibn Ishāq, op. cit., p. 546.

success constitute the core of Islamic theology as taught ever since in the sprawling seminaries. The principal lessons are two. The first is that Muslims should continue resorting to violence on any and every pretext till they triumph; setbacks are temporary. The second lesson is that Islam should refuse to coexist or compromise with every other religion and culture, and use the first favourable opportunity to wipe out the others completely so that it alone may prevail. Our present context is concerned with the second lesson.

THE PAGAN TEMPLE OF KA'BA

Soon after entering Mecca, the Prophet went to the Ka'ba, took its key from 'Uthmān B. Tālha, and entered it. Ibn Ishāq records, "There he found a dove made of wood. He broke it in his hands and threw it away." Next he turned to the idols which were housed in and around the temple. They were 360 in number. "The apostle was standing by them with a stick in his hand, saying, 'The truth has come and falsehood has passed away. Verily, falsehood is bound to pass away' (Sūra. 17.82).[21] Then he pointed at them with his stick and they collapsed on their backs one after the other. When the apostle prayed the noon prayer on the day of the conquest he ordered that all the idols which were round the Ka'ba should be collected and burned with fire and broken up. Faḍāla b. al-Mulāwwih al-Laythī said commemorating the day of the conquest:

Had you seen Muhammad and his troops
The day the idols were smashed when he entered,
You would have seen God's light become manifest
And darkness covering the face of idolatry."[22]

Another account says: "Biographical works are filled with the accounts of this proceeding, and that three hundred and sixty idols, the greatest whereof was Hobal, had been erected by the idolaters around the Ka'bah. In some copies we read that Eblis had fixed the bases of all these idols underground with lead, but that nevertheless when the apostle of Allah touched them with the lance or stick he had in his hands, and uttered the words: 'Truth had come, and falsehood has departed', the idols fell on their faces at the mere touch of the staff...There is a tradition ascribed to A'bdullah B. A'bbas that whenever his lordship pointed on that day to the face of an idol, the same immediately fell on its back, and whenever he pointed to the back it fell on its

---

[21]The verse was cited whenever Muslim invaders destroyed Hindu temples.
[22]Ibid., op. cit., p. 552.

face."[23]

The Islamic lore has thus turned into a miracle what was actually a show of brute physical force. "Muhammad when he entered Mekka as victor is stated to have struck them in the eyes with his bow before he had them dragged down and destroyed by fire."[24] The burning of the idols gave rise to another story in Islamic lore. "Upon the conquest of Mecca the Prophet cut open some of these idols with his sword and black smoke is said to have issued forth from them, a sign of the psychic influence which had made these idols their dwelling place."[25] One wonders what else except smoke could have come out when objects made of stone and wood were burnt. It is the privilege of Islamic lore to invest smoke with psychic power.

Hubal, the principal idol in the Ka'ba "was pulled down and used as a doorstep when the Prophet conquered Mecca and purified the Ka'bah."[26] This particular practice of the Prophet set up a pious precedent which was followed extensively when Islamic iconoclasm arrived in India. Many Hindu idols ended at the doorsteps of the principal mosques not only in Muslim capitals within India such as Ghazni, Kabul, Lahore, Multan, Nagore, Ajmer, Delhi, Jaunpur, Gaur, Daulatabad, Mandu, Ahmadabad, Gulbarga, Bidar, Bijapur, Ahmadnagar, Golkunda, Dhaka and Murshidabad, but also in far off places like Baghdad, Mecca and Medina, "The other stones which were worshipped as idols were actually used as corner-stones of the Ka'ba and as such we must consider also the Maqām Ibrāhīm."[27] This too was a pious precedent which was followed extensively in India. A large number of mosques and other Muslim monuments in India have Hindu idols or their pieces embedded in their masonry.

There was only one idol which the Prophet not only spared but also consecrated with his kiss so that every Muslim who performs Hajj is expected to do the same. This was the black stone now described pompously as al-Ḥajar al-Aṣwad. The Muslims present on the occasion felt puzzled by the Prophet's partiality for this particular stone. They were informed that the black stone had descended directly from heaven. According to a well-known tradition (*hadīth*) from Ibn'Abbās, the Prophet told his people, "By Allāh, Allāh will lift it up on the Last Day. It will have two eyes with which it will see. It will have a tongue with

[23] *The Rauzat-us-Safa*, op. cit., Vol. II, pt. II, p. 599.
[24] *First Encyclopaedia of Islam*, op. cit., Vol. VII, p. 147.
[25] Cyril Glasse *The Concise Encyclopaedia of Islam*, London, 1987, p. 179.
[26] Ibid., p. 160.
[27] *First Encyclopaedia of Islam*. op. cit., Vol. VII, pp. 147-48.

which it will speak and stand witness for that man who had kissed it earnestly."[28] Other people's idols are stones, while one's own stone is God's spokesman! Many of his followers must have remained unimpressed by the mysterious pronouncement. A few years later, Caliph 'Umar (AD 632–44), while kissing the black stone, is reported to have said, "I know that you are a stone which can neither help nor hurt. I would not have kissed you, had I not witnessed the Prophet of Allāh kissing you."[29]

Idols were not the only "abominations" which the Prophet had to take care of in the Ka'ba. Ibn Ishāq and other biographers of the Prophet report that the "Quraysh had put pictures in the Ka'ba including two of Jesus son of Mary and Mary...The apostle ordered that the pictures would be erased except those of Jesus and Mary."[30] According to a tradition, as 'Umar began to wash out the pictures with the water of the well known as Zamzam, "Muhammad placed his hand on the pictures of Jesus and Mary and said, 'Wash out all except what is below my hands.' He then withdrew his hand."[31] There is no reason to doubt that the walls of the Ka'ba carried paintings. Pagans have always been as fond of presenting their pantheon and mythology through colour as through carving. But it is pure invention that the paintings included those of Jesus and Mary. The Pagans who had maintained the Ka'ba and decorated its walls with paintings were not only not enamoured of the Christian god and his mother, they actually entertained abhorrence for them. Allāh himself says in the Qur'ān that the disbelievers show disrespect for Īsā. Referring to 'Umar's act of effacing the paintings, Margoliouth observes, "Whom or what they represented we know only on Mohammed's authority, which we are not inclined to trust..."[32]

Scholars have made several speculations regarding the Prophet's attitude to the Ka'ba. Basing themselves on legends found in the biographies of the Prophet, some say that he had reverence for the national sanctuary but regretted its misuse by the Pagans. Some others say that when he changed the Qibla from the Temple in Jerusalem to the Ka'ba in Mecca, he did so in order to conciliate Arab national sentiment. "We do not know the personal feelings of the youthful Muhammad towards the Ka'ba and the Meccan cult, but they were presumably of a conventional nature. What the biography of the Prophet tells us about his

[28] Translated from the Urdu version of *Mishkāt Sharīf*, Delhi, (n.d.), Vol. I, p. 572.
[29] Ibid., p. 574.
[30] Ibn Ishāq, op. cit., p. 552.
[31] *First Encyclopaedia of Islam*, op. cit., Vol. IV, p. 587.
[32] D.S. Margoliouth, op. cit. p. 387.

Meccan period in this respect can lay no claim to historical value. The Meccan revelations tell us nothing about these relations during the important period in the life of the Prophet. In any case, he felt no enthusiam for the Meccan sanctuary."[33]

In fact, there is a tradition that he wanted to destroy the Ka'ba. 'Ā'isha has reported him as saying to her that "if your people had not renounced ignorance promptly and become Musalmans, I would have demolished the Ka'ba and rebuilt it with two doors."[34] The tradition seems to be authentic because it inspired demolition and rebuilding of the Ka'ba on two subsequent occasions. "When A'bdullah Bin Zobeir heard this tradition he destroyed the building of the Qoraish whilst he held sway, and rebuilt the Ka'bah according to the intentions of his lordship the last of the prophets. When, however, Hajjāj Bin Yusuf undertook by order of A'bd-ul-Malik Merwān [AD 685–705] a compaign against A'bdullah Bin Zobeir and vanquished him, he destroyed the edifice built by the latter at the command of the same Khalifah and re-erected it as the Qoraish had built it during the lifetime of his holy and prophetic lordship. When Harūn-ur-Rashid became Khalifah he desired to annihilate the edifice of Merwān, and to rebuild the Ka'bah according to the model of A'bdullah Bin Zobeir. On this subject he consulted the Imām Mālek, but the latter replied: 'O commander of the faithful, let the Ka'bah alone, let it not become the sport of kings.' Accordingly Harūn renounced his intention."[35]

What was this "building of the Qoreish" which Ibn Zubayr demolished and Hajjāj restored? This much is clear from Muslim accounts that it was a pagan temple housing the idols of many Gods. These acconts, however, insist that in the ancient past it was a place of monotheistic worship consecrated by Abraham. There is only one Muslim account which preserves a pagan tradition. "According to al-Mas'ūdī (Murūdj, iv, 47), certain people have regarded the Ka'ba as a temple devoted to the sun, the moon and the five planets. The 360 idols placed round the Ka'ba also point in the same direction. It can therefore hardly be denied that traces exist of an astral symbolism..."[36] That the Ka'ba was a centre of sun-worship is also confirmed by whatever memories of the pre-Islamic Hajj survive in Muslim accounts. "As soon as the sun was visible, the *ifāḍa* to Minā used to begin in pre-Islamic times. Mu-

---

[33] *First Encyclopaedia of Islam*, Vol. IV, p,. 587

[34] Translated from the Urdu version of *Jāmi' Tirmizi*, New Delhi, 1983, Vol. I, p. 330.

[35] *The Rauzat-us-Safa*, op. cit., Vol. I, pt. II, p. 133.

[36] *First Encyclopaedia of Islam*, op. cit., Vol. IV, p. 591.

hammad therefore ordained that this should begin before sunrise; here again we have the attempt to destroy a solar rite. In ancient times they are said to have sung during the *ifāḍa, ashrīq thabīr kaimā nughīr*. The explanation of these words is uncertain; it is sometimes translated: 'Enter into light of morning, Thabir, so that we may hasten.'"[37]

It is pointed out by apologists of Islam that the Prophet did not convert the pagan temple into a mosque and that he only "restored" it to what it used to be in Abraham's time. We known that the Abraham story about the Ka'ba is a fabrication floated after the Prophet had left Mecca and quarrelled with the Jews of Medina. And there was no specific architectural design for a mosque developed during the lifetime of the Prophet; any structure, in any shape could serve the purpose. For the rest, everything that needs be done for depriving a place of its pagan character and converting it into a place of Islamic worship, was done by the Prophet. The conversion of the temple at Mecca into a mosque was complete when Bilāl stood on the roof of the Ka'ba and recited *aẕān*.

IDOLS IN MECCA

In Mecca proper, Isāf and Nā'ila were the only other important idols outside the Ka'ba. They were the deities of as-Safa and al-Marwah. "On that occasion the lord of apostleship ordered A'li...to break to pieces Asāf and Nāylah...When these two idols were broken a rude black woman issued from one of them, when his holy and prophetic lordship said: 'This is Nāylah. But she will never any more be worshipped in your country.'"[38]

At the same time, "The proclaimer authorised by the apostle of Allāh went throughout Mecca calling upon all those who believe in Allāh and the Last Day to leave no idol unbroken in their homes."[39]

Having "purified" Mecca, the Prophet sent "expeditions to those idols which were in the neighbourhood and had them destroyed; these included al-'Uzzā, Manāt, Suwā', Buāna and Dhu'l-Kaffayn."[40]

THE PAGAN TEMPLE OF AL-'UZZĀ

"Then the apostle sent Khālid to al-'Uzzā which was in Nakhla. It was a temple which the tribe of Quraysh and Kināna and all Muḍar

---

[37] Ibid., Vol., III, p. 200. We shall deal with this subject further in the Appendix.
[38] *The Rauzat-us-Safa,* op. cit., Vol. II, pt. II, p. 599.
[39] *Tabqāt-i-Ibn Sa'd,* op. cit., p. 478. See also Martin Ling, *Muhammad,* Rochester, (Vermont, USA), 1983, p. 301.
[40] Ibid.

used to venerate. Its guardians were B. Shaybān of B. Sulaym, allies of B. Hāshim. When the Sulamī guardian heard of Khālid's coming he hung his sword on her, climbed the mountain on which she stood, and said:

> O'Uzzā, make an annihilating attack on Khālid,
> Throw aside your veil and gird up your train.
> O 'Uzzā, if you do not kill this man Khālid
> Then bear a swift punishment or become a Christian.

When Khālid arrived he destroyed her and returned to the apostle."[41] It is significant that the pagan priest saw no difference between becoming a Muslim and becoming a Christian.

The rest of the story is told in other sources. "He [the Prophet] asked him [Khālid], 'Did you see anything?' Khālid replied, 'Nothing.' He [the Prophet] said, 'Go again, and smash her to pieces.' Khālid went back, demolished the building in which the idol was housed, and started smashing the idol itself. The [pagan] priest raised a cry, 'O 'Uzzā, manifest your might.' All of a sudden a nude and dishevelled black woman came out of that idol. Khālid cut her down with his sword and took possession of the jewels and ornaments she wore. He reported the proceedings to the Prophet who observed. 'That was 'Uzzā. She will be worshipped no more.'"[42] There is a tradition that when the expedition was sent to Nakhla for the destruction of al-'Uzzā, the Prophet instructed Khālīd, "In whatever settlement you do not hear the *azān* or see no mosque, slaughter the people of that place."[43]

THE PAGAN TEMPLE OF SUWĀ'

"The apostle of Allāh sent 'Amr b. al-'Ās towards [the temple of] Suwā', the idol of Huḍayl, in order to destroy it. When 'Amr arrived there, the priest [of the temple] asked him, 'What do you want?' 'Amr replied, 'The apostle of Allāh has commanded me to destroy this idol.' He [the priest]said, 'You cannot overpower him.' 'Amr asked, 'Why?' He [the priest] said, 'He is well-protected.' 'Amr said. 'You subscribe to falsehood even now? May you perish! Does he hear or see?' 'Amr approached the idol and smashed it. Then he ordered his companions to demolish the house which contained [the temple's] treasure. That house yielded nothing."[44]

---

[41] Ibn Ishāq, op. cit., p. 565.
[42] *Tārikh-i-Tabari,* op. cit., pp. 404–05.
[43] *Tabqāt-i-Ibn Sa'd,* op. cit., p. 488.
[44] Ibid., p. 85.

THE PAGAN TEMPLE OF AL-MANĀT

"The expedition to Manāt was sent under Sa'd b. Zayd al-Ashahlī in the Ramzān of AH 8.... It was the idol of Ghassān, Aws and Khazraj in al-Mushallal...Sa'd started with twenty cavalrymen and reached there at a time when the priest was in attendance. The priest asked them, 'What do you want?' They said, 'Destruction of Manāt.' The priest exclaimed, 'You, and want to do this!' Sa'd approached the idol. A black and nude and dishevelled woman came out and advanced towards him, cursing and beating her breast. The priest said, 'O Manāt, manifest your might.' Sa'd started hitting her, and she was cut down. He had asked his companions to take care of the idol in the meanwhile. They smashed it. But the treasury yielded nothing,"[45] Other sources attribute the destruction of the sanctuary of Manāt in Qudayd to 'Alī bin Abū Tālib, still others to Abū Sufyān.[46] It is most likely that more than one temple of Manāt was destroyed.

THE SACRED TREE

Soon after the occupation of Mecca, the Prophet had to face a formidable alliance of pagan tribes that had assembled in the valley of Hunayn between Mecca and Tā'if. Ibn Ishāq records a tradition from Hārith b. Mālik: "We went forth with the apostle to the Hunayn fresh from paganism. The heathen Quraysh and other Arabs had a great green tree Dhātu Anwāt to which they used to come every year and hang their weapons on it and sacrifice beside it and devote themselves to it for a day." As the newly converted pagans saw that tree, they said to the Prophet, "Make us a tree to hang things on such as they have." The Prophet chided them, comparing them to the people of Moses who wanted the latter to "make us a god even as they have gods."[47] It is not recorded whether the sacred tree was cut down at that time. Perhaps the Prophet was in a hurry. But it is a safe bet that the tree was marked for destruction.

The army of Islam suffered a severe setback in the first round of the Battle of Hunayn. The newly converted Pagans were overjoyed. Abū Sufyān, when he saw the Muslims in headlong flight, observed, "They will not stop till they reach the seashore." A pagan who had been granted respite from conversion for a specified period asked, "Has not sorcery [Islam] come to an end today?"[48]

---

[45] Ibid., pp. 485–86.
[46] *First Encyclopaedia of Islam*, op. cit., Vol. V, pp. 231-32.
[47] Ibn Ishāq, op. cit., pp. 568–69.
[48] *Tārikh-i-Tabari*, op. cit., p. 413.

The Prophet himself was in great danger. The situation was saved by lack of tactical skill on the pagan side. They failed to pursue the demoralised Muslim army, and were defeated by the counter-attack which followed after the Muslims managed to regroup. The remnants of their defeated allies took refuge in the fortified town of Tā'if. A Muslim poetess sang:

Allah's cavalry has beaten Al-Lāt's cavalry,
And Allah best deserves to hold fast.[49]

Al-Lāt was the chief Goddess of the allied pagan tribes, and had a renowned sanctuary in Tā'if. So the army of Islam advanced towards this town.

THE PAGAN TEMPLE OF DHU'L KAFFAYN

On the way to Tā'if the Prophet detached Tufayl b. 'Amr al-Dausī and sent him to destroy the temple of Dhu'l Kaffayn. It was maintained by 'Amar's own tribe of Daus. He was to rejoin the main army after accomplishing the assignment. "He moved fast towards his people, and destroyed Dhu'l Kaffayn. As he set fire to the idol, starting from its face, he said:

O Dhu'l Kaffayn! we are not of those that obey you,
Our birth goes back much prior to your own.
See, I have stuffed your heart with fire.

Four hundred men from his tribe followed him when he went back to the Prophet."[50]

The army of Islam was full of confidence when it arrived outside Tā'if. The court poet of the Prophet, Ka'b b. Mālik, sang:

Al-Lāt and Al-'Uzzā and Wudd are forgotten,
And we plunder them of their necklaces and earings.

And Shaddād b. 'Āriḍ al-Jushamī said:

Don't help Al-Lāt for God is about to destroy her
How can one who cannot help herself he helped?[51]

But the boast proved empty and al-Lāt survived on this occasion. Tā'if proved a hard nut to crack. "When he found the gates closed and determined resistance offered, he endeavoured to frighten the Thakafites by a wholesale destruction of their property. This was how he had dealt with the Banu Nadir. But the Thakafites were no Jews."[52] The

---

[49] Ibn Ishāq, op. cit., p. 572.
[50] *Tabqāt-i-Ibn Sa'd,* op. cit., p. 496.
[51] Ibn Ishāq, op. cit., p. 588.
[52] D.S. Margoliouth, op. cit., p. 404.

siege had to be raised, though newly acquired heavy war-engines had been employed for battering the city walls.

THE PAGAN TEMPLES AROUND TĀ'IF

The only satisfaction the Prophet could derive during his siege of Tā'if was from what he got done in the environs. He "ordered his glorious companions to fell the date-trees and to destroy the vineyards of the neighbourhood," which acts were considered serious crimes according to the ethics of pagan warfare. The Prophet had learnt the art of total war from the Judaic and Christian scriptures. He also indulged in his most favourite pastime. "It is related in some biographies that while the siege of Tāyf was being carried on, his holy and prophetic lordship appointed A'li Murtadza with a number of glorious companions to make excursions into the country, and to destroy every idol they could find...Thereon A'li, the Commander of the Faithful...destroyed all the idols of the Bani Hoāzān and Bani Thaqyf which were in that region. The apostle was waiting for his return near the gate of the fort of Tāyf, and as soon as the prince of saints had terminated his business, he joined the august camp, was received by the seal of prophets with the exclamation of the Takbyr..."[53] No count of temples destroyed is available in the sources. They must have been many. Islamic invaders of India followed the example whenever they besieged a town; they destroyed all gardens and groves and places of worship around it.

THE MOSQUE OF OPPOSITION

"The apostle went on until he stopped in Dhū Awān a town an hour's light journey from Medina. The owners of the mosque of opposition had come to the apostle as he was preparing for Tabūk saying, 'We have built a mosque for the sick and needy and for nights of bad weather, and we should like you to come to us and pray for us there.' He said that he was on the point of travelling, and was preoccupied, or words to that effect, and that when he came back he would come to them and pray for them in it.

"When he stopped in Dhū Awān news of the mosque came to him, and he summoned Mālik b. al-Dukhshum...and Ma'n b. 'Adīy...and told them to go to the mosque of those evil men and destroy and burn it. They went quickly to B. Sālim b. 'Auf who were Mālik's clan, and Mālik said to Ma'n, 'Wait for me until I can bring fire from my

---

[53] *The Rauzat-us-Safa,* op. cit., Vol. II, pt. II, pp. 630–31. *Takbīr* is the Muslim war-cry, *Allāhu Akbar*.

people.' So he went in and took a palm-branch and lighted it, and then the two of them ran into the mosque where its people were and burned and destroyed it and the people ran away from it."[54]

The sources offer no evidence that this mosque was built on land acquired illegitimately, as apologists of Islam like Ashgar Ali Engineer and some Hindu leaders have been saying in the context of the Rāmajanmabhūmi controversy. The only point which emerges is that it was built by Muslims who did not see eye to eye with Muhammad. Margoliouth observes: "Of the rights and wrongs of this affair nothing decided will ever be known: the revelation in which it is mentioned,[55] and which contains a variety of oracles delivered in connection with the expedition to Tabuk, is in a tone of bitterness and vexation such as disappointment and opposition are likely to engender in a man of Mohammed's temperament. The people of Medinah and their new Bedouin allies are charged with harbouring Hypocrites: and it also appears that the Koran was beginning to give rise to criticism from which the Prophet had suffered at Meccah. When a new revelation comes down, people at Medinah ask each other sarcastically whether their faith had been increased. Knots of people are found talking and laughing: inspite of the most earnest denials, the Prophet is of the opinion that the Koran has provided the materials for their amusement...There is also one verse in the tirade suggesting that some of the malcontents disliked the plan of living on plunder which was now characteristic of Islam, and wished a more honest system inaugurated..."[56]

Obviously, the mosque of opposition was built by people who were monotheists like Muhammad but who did not believe that the doctrine enjoined murder and rapine which had become the Muslims' daily practice. Small wonder that Allāh of the Qur'ān who sanctioned mass slaughter and endless accumulation of plunder by the faithful, did not approve of such "toothless" monotheism. So he moaned, "Is he who founded his building upon duty to Allāh and his good pleasure better; or he who founded his building on the brink of a crumbling, overhanging precipice so that it toppled with him into the fire of hell?"[57] It was not for nothing that Allāh of the Qur'ān was known as *al-Zarr*, the Distresser, and as *al-Mughnī*, the Enricher, that is, by means of booty.

---

[54] Ibn Ishāq, op. cit., p. 609.

[55] Qur'ān, Sūra 9. This is the last Sūra of Qur'ān, speaking chronologically. It shows the frustration of Muhammad at the failure of his mission. Allāh says that most people who had converted to Islam were hypocrites, that is, Pagans at heart.

[56] D.S. Margoliouth, op. cit., pp. 424–45.

[57] Qur'ān, 9.109.

INVITATIONS TO ISLAM

The occupation of Mecca had sky-rocketted the prestige of the Prophet. "In deciding their attitude to Islam," writes Ibn Ishāq, "the Arabs were only waiting to see what happened to the clan of Quraysh and the apostle. For Quraysh were the leaders and guides of men, the people of the sacred temple, and the pure stock of Ishmael son of Abraham; and the leading Arabs did not contest this. It was Quraysh who had declared war on the apostle and opposed him; and when Mecca was occupied and Quraysh became subject to him and he subdued it to Islam, and the Arabs knew that they could not fight the apostle or display enmity towards him they entered into God's religion 'in batches' as God said,[58] coming to him from all directions."[59] Muhammad's war-machine was sending waves of terror towards all tribes, which was a very effective message. There was a debate afoot everywhere whether to fight for the ancient religion and tribal honour, or submit to Muhammad and become Muslim. The Prophet's intelligence network kept him informed of what was happening where. He was swift in exploiting the psychological crisis to his own advantage.

The groundwork had been done during the preceding two years. Ibn Sa'd provides a list of tribal chiefs to whom the Prophet had sent invitations to Islam, starting soon after the Treaty of Hudaybiya with the Meccans in the year AH 6.[60] The letters containing his messages were carried by special couriers selected from among his companions. The message varied according to the status and strength of the tribe concerned. Unfortunately, Ibn Sa'd has lumped together the invitations without regard for chronological sequence. This much, however, can be inferred that their tone became sharper as the author of the messages marched from one victory to another, the acme being reached in the conquest of Mecca and the Battle of Hunayn.

At first Muhammad wrote his letters beginning with *basmak al-Laham*, "I begin in the name of Allāh," after the custom of the Quraysh. A special revelation came and he was commanded to begin with *bismallāh*, "In the name of Allāh." Another revelation amended the formula to *bismallāh al-Raḥmān al-Raḥīm*, "In the name of Allāh, the Compassionate, the Merciful." Finally, it was revealed to him that he should begin with *bismallāh al-Raḥīm al-Waḥīd*, "In the name of

[58] Ibid., Sūra 110.

[59] Ibn Ishāq, op. cit., p. 628. Reference to Abraham and Ishmael may be ignored as concoctions.

[60] *Tabqāt-i-Ibn Sa'd*, op.cit., Part II, pp. 29–64.

Allāh, the Compassionate, the One."[61] Monotheism of Islam had to be emphasized.

The general tenor of the messages sent was the same—dissociate from the idolaters which meant an order to destroy pagan temples and break idols; bear witness that Allāh is one without partners and Muhammad is his messenger which meant submission to Muhammad; establish prayers which meant an order to build mosques; pay *zakāt* and other taxes to the central treasury at Medina which meant contribution to Muhammad's treasury; send to the Prophet one-fifth of the plunder obtained from raids on the polytheists which meant an order to plunder the Pagans; and keep the highways free from disturbance so that Muslim delegations can travel unmolested for converting people and collecting taxes. In exchange, the tribes were assured that they could keep their lands, their cattle, their wells, their gardens, their houses, and such of their special customs as did not come in conflict with Islam. Defiance, they were warned, would entail slaughter of their men, capture of their women and children, and laying waste of their country. And punitive expeditions were sent to those tribal settlements which resisted the Prophet's messengers or otherwise refused to abide by his dictates.[62] The fear was abroad that "the Prophet of Allāh may send a military force."[63] When Banī Tamīm refused to pay *zakāt,* they were attacked, and eleven of their women and thirty of their children were captured and dragged to Medina."[64]

THE YEAR OF DEPUTATIONS

"When the apostle had gained possession of Mecca," reports Ibn Ishāq, "and had finished with Tabūk, and Thaqīf had surrendered and paid homage, deputations from the Arabs came to him from all directions."[65] Ibn Sa'd lists as many as seventy-one deputations which waited on Muhammad in Medina, the last one being on behalf of the wolves.[66] It seems that the beasts felt that they, too, could confess the faith without suffering any inconvenience.

A deputation came to Muhammad from Tā'if soon after he had suffered a repulse outside that city. It seems that the morale of the people in this town collapsed as they saw what was happening all

---

[61] Ibid., p. 35.
[62] Ibid., p. 53.
[63] Ibid., p. 62.
[64] Ibid., p. 67.
[65] Ibn Ishāq, op. cit., p. 627.
[66] *Tabqāt-i-Ibn Sa'd,* op. cit., Vol. II, pp. 64–136.

around. The deputation met Muhammad even before he had reached Medina. It was led by 'Urwa b. Mas'ūd al-Thaqafī who was one of the leaders of resistance when Tā'if was besieged by the army of Islam. 'Urwa requested Muhammad to make him a Muslim so that he could go back and invite his people to the true faith. He was baptised and sent back. But "when he went up to an upper room and showed his religion to them they shot arrows at him from all directions, and one hit him and killed him."[67]

The debate in Tā'if, however, did not come to an end. One of their chiefs said, "We are in an impasse. You have seen how the affair of this man has progressed. All the Arabs have accepted Islam and you lack the power to fight them, so look to your ease...So after conferring together they dicided to send a man to the apostle as they had sent 'Urwa..."[68] The man approached for the job refused to go alone. Finally a deputation consisting of six chiefs reached Medina and met the Prophet.

THE PAGAN TEMPLE OF AL-LĀT

"Among the things they [chiefs from Tā'if] asked the apostle was that they should be allowed to retain their idol Al-Lāt undestroyed for three years. The apostle refused, and they continued to ask him for a year or two, and he refused; finally they asked for a month after their return home, but he refused to agree to any set time. All that they wanted as they were trying to show was to be safe from their fanatics and women and children by leaving her, and they did not want to frighten their people by destroying her until they had accepted Islam. The apostle refused this...They had also asked that he would excuse them from prayer and they should not have to break their idols with their own hands. The apostle said: 'We excuse you from breaking your idols with your own hands, but as for prayer there is no good in a religion which has no prayers.' They said that they would perform them though it was demeaning...

"When they had accomplished their task and had set out to return to their country the apostle sent with then Abū Sufyān and al-Mughīra to destroy their idol.They travelled with the deputation and when they neared al-Tā'if, al-Mughīra wanted to send on Abū Sufyān in advance. The latter refused and told him to go to his people while he stayed in the property of Dhū'l-Ḥaram.[69] When al-Mughīra entered he went up to

[67] Ibn Ishāq, op. cit., p. 614.
[68] Ibid., 615.
[69] Al-Mughīra belonged to Tā'if and was an earlier convert.

the idol and struck it with a pick-axe. His people the B. Mu'attib stood in front of him fearing that he would be shot or killed as 'Urwa had been. The women of Thaqīf came out with their heads uncovered bewailing her and saying:

O weep for our protector
Poltroons would neglect her
Whose swords need a corrector.

Abū Sufyān, as al-Mughīra smote her with the axe, said, 'Alas for you, alas !' When al-Mughīra had destroyed her and taken what was on her and her jewels he sent for Abū Sufyān when her jewellery and gold and beads had been collected.

"Now Abū Mulayḥ b. 'Urwa and Qārib b. al-Aswad had come to the apostle before the Thaqīf deputation when 'Urwa was killed, desiring to separate themselves from Thaqīf and to have nothing to do with them...'Urwa asked the apostle to settle a debt his father had incurred from the property of the idol.The apostle agreed and Qārib b. al-Aswad asked for the same privilege for his father...The apostle said, 'But al-Aswad died a polytheist.' He answered, 'But you will be doing a favour to a Muslim a near relation,' meaning himself...The apostle ordered Abū Sufyān to satisfy the debts of 'Urwa and al-Aswad from the property of the idol..."[70]

The account shows that the people of Tā'if accepted Islam under duress. It also shows the stuff of which the voluntary converts to Islam like 'Urwa and al-Aswad were made. Most of them were questionable characters. The story has been the same wherever Islam has spread. It is only the subsequent generations of Muslims who suffer from loss of memory.

THE PAGAN TEMPLES OF B. SA'D B. BAKR

They sent their chief, Ḍimām b. Tha'laba, to the Prophet. Ḍimām asked some questions and ended by becoming a Muslim. He went back to his people and said, "How evil are al-Lāt and al-'Uzzā!" His people rebuked him, "Heavens above, Ḍimām, beware of leprosy and elephantiasis and madness!" He replied, "Woe to you, they can neither hurt nor heal. God has sent an apostle and sent down to him a book, so seek deliverance thereby from your present state..."[71] He then destroyed the idols "It was not yet evening that day that all men and women became Muslamans. They built mosques and recited *azāns* so that people came

[70] Ibn Ishāq, op. cit., pp. 615–17.
[71] Ibid., p. 635.

to prayers."[72]

THE PAGAN TEMPLE OF B. SULAYM

Seven hundred people from B. Sulaym had waited on the Prophet while he was in Qudayd on his way to Mecca, which he occupied soon after. They went to him again after the conquest of Mecca, Battle of Hunayn and the siege of Tā'if. Their leader Ghādī b. 'Abd al-'Uzzā was the keeper of their temple. The Prophet bestowed upon him the estate of Rehātā which had a spring in it. He came back and composed the following couplets about the idol he had worshipped earlier:

How can that be God, on whom
The foxes came and staled?
He is abominable without a doubt,
He on whom the foxes staled.

He attacked the idol and smashed it to pieces. When he waited upon the Prophet with this report, he was asked, "What is your name?" He said, "Ghādī 'Abd al-'Uzzā." The Prophet said, "You are Rāshid b. 'Abd Raba."[73] People whose names referred to pagan Gods were always given new names by the Prophet—names which referred to the god of Islam.

THE CHRISTIAN CHURCH OF YAMĀMA

A deputation of nineteen men from B. Hanīfa came to Medina. They were given rich food and instructed in Islam by the Prophet. Each of them was given five ounces of silver as a gift. When they got ready to go back, the Prophet gave them a vessel of water with which he had performed his ablutions. He said, "When you return to your country, destroy the church, wash the site with water, and build a mosque on it." They did accordingly. The priest in charge of the church ran away. His days were over.[74]

THE PAGAN TEMPLES OF FILS AND RUḌĀ'

"The Prophet sent 'Alī b. Abī Tālib towards the temple of Fils belonging to the tribe of Tayy, with an order to destroy it...He went with two hundred horsemen..."[75]

"'Alī inflicted atrocities on them and took prisoners from among them. He obtained two swords from the temple; one of them was

[72] *Tabqāt-t-Ibn-Sa'd*, op. cit., Vol. II, p. 73.
[73] Ibid., p. 81.
[74] Ibid., p. 90 91.
[75] Ibid., p. 97.

named Rasūb, the other Makhzam. It was well-known that these swords had been brought as an offering to the temple by Hārith b. Abī Thamar. Among the prisoners was a sister of 'Adi b. Hātim..."[76] Hātim Tayy, the father of the girl, was a pagan chief renowned for his liberality. Islamic lore tells many stories about him without revealing that he was a Pagan. The temple of Fils which was destroyed was on Mount Aja'. Another deity of Tayy was Ruḍā'.[77] His temple, too, met the same fate.

THE PAGAN TEMPLE OF 'AMM ANAS

A deputation consisting of ten men came to Medina from Khaulan in the year AH 10. They informed the Prophet that they were Muslims. The Prophet asked, "What about your idol of 'Amm Anas?" They replied, "That is in a bad shape. We have exchanged him for Allāh whom you have brought. When we go back, we shall destroy him." They were instructed in Islam and entertained lavishly. After a few days, the Prophet ordered that each of them be given twelve and a half ounces of silver as reward. They went back and destroyed the idol of 'Amm Anas "even before they untied their luggage."[78] It is not unoften that bribes bring quick results.

THE PAGAN TEMPLE OF 'UZRA

A deputation of twelve men from B.'Uzra came to Medina and said to the Prophet, "We are worried about our people." The Prophet instructed them in Islam and gave them gifts. He was told that the idol of 'Uzra had spoken and confirmed his prophethood. He observed, "This seems to be a believing jinn."[79] Idols, too, it seems, could become believers. It is not recorded whether this particular idol was kept or removed.

THE PAGAN TEMPLE OF AL-JAHĪNA

'Amr b. Marrah al-Jahnī relates, "We had an idol which we used to honour. I was its keeper. When I heard of the Prophet, I destroyed it. Then I went to Medina and became a Muslim. I composed the following verse:

I bear witness that Allāh is true,
I am the first to renounce stone idols."[80]

---

[76] *Tārīkh-i-Tabarī,* op. cit., p. 445.
[77] *First Encyclopaedia of Islam,* op. cit., Vol. II, p. 624.
[78] *Tabqāt-i-Ibn Sa'd,* op. cit., Vol. II, p. 100.
[79] Ibid., p. 107.
[80] Ibid., p. 109.

THE PAGAN TEMPLE OF FARRĀZ

Ḍbab, a man from the tribe of Sa'd al-Ashīra attacked the idol named Farrāz and smashed it to pieces. He went with a deputation to the Prophet and said:

I became a follower of the Prophet
When he brought (good) intructions.
I consigned Farrāz to a status of dishonour,
I attacked him and left him in a state
As if he never existed; this is the time of revolution.[81]

THE PAGAN TEMPLE OF DHU'L-KHALAṢA

Jarīr b. 'Abd-allāh al-Bahlī came to Medina with one hundred and fifty men. All of them professed Islam. The Prophet asked Jarīr about those whom he had left behind. Jarīr replied, "O apostle of Allah! Allah has made Islam dominant among them. *Azān* prevails from mosques and courtyards. They have destroyed the idols they used to worship." The Prophet asked, "What happened to the idol of Dhu'l Khalaṣa?" He was told, "He is as before. Allāh willing, we will be rid of him." The Prophet sent them back. Jarīr returned before long and reported, "I have destroyed the idol and taken whatever it wore. I set fire to it and reduced it to such a state that whoever had honoured him will now hate him. No one stopped us from doing this."[82]

"It is reported that after the burning and destruction of the idol-temple the inhabitants of Dhu'l-Khalasa attained the nobility of Islam. The treasury belonging to that temple contained much property and perfumes, all of which was brought to Medinah. When his holy and prophetic lordship heard what had taken place, and that the idol-temple had been demolished, he rejoiced greatly, inviting a benediction on Jaryr and his tribe..."[83]

"Some of the idols were made use of for other purposes, as for example the idol of Dhu'l-Khalaṣa, a white piece of marble in which a crown was carved and which was worshipped at Tabāla, a place on the road from Mekka to Yaman, was in the time of Ibn al-Kalbī (about AH 200) used as a stepping-stone under the mosque at Ṭabāla..."[84]

THE PAGAN TEMPLE OF RUḌĀ'

It was the temple of B. Rabī'a, a branch of B. Tamīm. Al-Mus-

---

[81] Ibid., p. 118.
[82] Ibid., pp. 123–24.
[83] *The Rauzat-us-Safa,* op. cit., Vol. II, pt. II, pp. 677–79.
[84] *First Encyclopaedia Islam,* op. cit., Vol. VII, p. 147.

taughir b. Rabī'a, a man of the same tribe, destroyed it. He sang:

I smashed Ruḍā' so completely that
I left it a black ruin in a hollow.[85]

SUMMING UP

Surveying the scene in the year of deputations, Margoliouth sums up, "The iconoclasm which had raged at Medinah at the time of the Prophet's arrival spread far and wide, now it had been clearly proved that the old gods were incapable of defending themselves or of even taking revenge on those who broke them. Facts which had remained unheeded for generations suddenly began to suggest important inferences: one man observed that his god suffered himself to be desecrated by beasts, and declined henceforward to worship a deity on whom the foxes staled. The persons who hurry to place their incense on the altar of success are familiar figures in all ages: and many a comedy was enacted at these visits..."[86]

CONCLUSION

Thus the practices of the Prophet or his Sunnah vis-a-vis idols and idol-temples was added to prescriptions of the Qur'ān in this respect, and the Islamic theology of iconoclasm stood completed. Ever since, iconoclasm has been a prominent as well a permanent part of the theology of Islam.

Allāh had denounced the idols and their worship as abominable. His prophet got the idols broken or burnt, and their temples destroyed.

The Prophet added a few nuances on his own. He got the sites and materials of pagan temples used in the construction of mosques that replaced them. In many cases, idols were placed on the footsteps of the mosques so that the faithful could trample upon them while entering and coming out of Allāh's abodes. These acts, too, became pious precedents and were followed by Islamic invaders wherever they came across idols.

THE PLACE OF SUNNAH IN ISLAM

People who have not studied the theology of Islam as expounded in orthodox treatises, believe that Islam stands for obedience to the commandments of Allāh as revealed in the Qur'ān. They do not know that Allāh is no more than mere window-dressing and that for all prac-

[85] Ibn Ishāq, op. cit., p. 39.
[86] D.S. Margoliouth, op. cit., pp. 431–32.

tical purposes the Prophet rules the roost.

Muhammad had made Allāh into his private preserve when he proclaimed that no one except him knew the will of Allāh first-hand, and that he alone will intercede on the Day of Judgment for deciding who will enter paradise and who will sink into hell. Going further, he made Allāh helplessly dependent on the Muslim *millat* when he prayed on the eve of the Battle of Badr, "O God, if this band perishes today, Thou will be worshipped no more."[87] This became a refrain in every Muslim prayer offered on the eve of every battle fought against the infidels in the history of Islam. Allāma Iqbal was not innovating when he addressed Allāh in his *Shikwah* and asked, "Did anyone before us bother about you?"

Muslims have a popular saying in Persian language, "*bā Khudā dīwānā bāsh wa bā Muhammad hoshiyār*," that is, one may become wild about Allāh but one should beware when it comes to Muhammad. *Khudā* is the Persian word for Allāh. Islam is, therefore, spelled out more correctly when it is called Muhammadanism. For, it is not Allāh but Muhammad who sits at the heart of Islam and controls its head as well.

The process of deifying the life-style of the Prophet had started in his own life-time. Margoliouth observes, "He inherited the devotion and adulation which had hitherto been bestowed on the idols; and though he never permitted the word worship to be used of the ceremonies of which he was the object, he ere long became hedged in with a state which differed little form that which surrounded a god..."[88] The concept of the Sunnah, that is, the practices of the Prophet, had also developed towards the end of his days.[89]

The very first sūfī illustrated what the Sunnah entailed. Farīdu'd-Dīn Attār gives the story of Uwaysh Qarnī who lived in the days of the Prophet but had never met or seen him. 'Umar and 'Alī were on a visit to Kufa when they learnt that Qarnī lived in the valley of 'Urfa, grazing cattle and eating dry bread. They went to see him. "The honourable Uwaysh said, 'You are Companions of the Prophet. Could you tell me which one of his sacred teeth was martyred in the Battle of Uhud? Why have you not broken all your teeth out of reverence for the Prophet?' This said, he opened his mouth and showed that all his teeth were gone. He explained, 'When I learnt that a tooth of the Prophet had been mar-

[87] *Sīrat Rasūl Allāh*, op. cit., p. 300.
[88] D.S. Margoliouth, op. cit., p. 216.
[89] *Sīrat Rasūl Allāh*, op. cit., p. 645–46

tyred, I broke one of mine. Then I thought that perhaps some other tooth of his had been martyred. So I broke all my teeth, one after another. It is only after that that I felt at peace'. Having heard him the two Companions got awe-struck, and felt convinced that this was the correct conduct..."[90]

The rightly-guided Caliphs who followed the Prophet regarded the Sunnah as a sure key to success. Quirks of history which gave many victories to the Muslim arms in the first century AH, convinced the theologians of Islam that the Sunnah was divine in its inspiration. They became busy in collecting and collating every detail of the Prophet's practices, from the act of coughing to that of waging holy wars and administrating what had become his exclusive kingdom. The Sunnah was soon placed on par with the Qur'ān. "In the Qur'ān," they propounded, "Allah speaks through Muhammad; in the *Sunnah,* He acts through him. Thus Muhammad's life is a visible expression of Allah's utterances in the Qur'ān. God provides the divine principle, Muhammad the living pattern."[91]

The Sunnah has been the prison-house in which the world of Islam has lived ever since. Every pious Muslim aspires to do things exactly as the Prophet did. Aping the Prophet in the matter of destroying other peoples places of worship, and building mosques with their materials is no exception. A Muslim who *can* do this pious deed but *does not* do it, disobeys the Prophet.

There are very few historical mosques, particularly Jāma' Masjids, in the world of Islam which do not stand on sites occupied earlier by other people's places of worship. Many Christian churches yielded place to mosques all over West Asia, North Africa, Spain and South-eastern Europe, even though Christians were People of the Book whose places of worship were to be protected once they agreed to become *zimmīs*. Fire-temples of the Zoroastrians suffered the same fate all over what constituted the empire of Iran on the eve of the Muslim conquest. The greatest havoc, however, was wrought in the vast cradle of Hindu culture where hundreds of thousands of Buddhist, Brahmanical, Jain and other Hindu temples disappeared or yielded place to mosques and other Muslim monuments.

Today there are no Hindu temples in the Central Asian republics of Russia, Sinkiang province of China, Makran and Seistan provinces of

---

[90] Shaykh Farīdu'd-Dīn Attār, *Tadhkirāt al-Awliyā'* translated into Urdu by Maulāna Zubayr Afzal Usmānī, Delhi n.d., p. 16.

[91] Ram Swarup, *Understanding Islam through Hadis: Religious Faith or Fanaticism?,* Voice of India, New Delhi, Second Reprint, 1987, p. vii.

Iran, and the whole of Afghanistan, all of which were honeycombed with them before the advent of Islam. Whatever Hindu temples had come up during the Sikh and British rule in what are now known as Pakistan and Bangladesh, are fast disappearing. The same has been happenning in the valley of Kashmir.

The Archaeological Survey of India, which included Pakistan and Bangladesh till 1947, has identified many mosques and other Muslim monuments which stand on the sites of Hindu temples and/or have temple materials embedded in their masonry. Many inscriptions in Arabic and Persian bear testimony that Hindu temples were destroyed for constructing mosques. Local traditions can point out many more mosques which have replaced Hindu temples. Cartloads of Hindu idols are known to have been brought and placed on the steps of the Jāmi' Masjids in several cities which were Muslim capitals at one time. Some of those idols may still be buried under the stairs of the same mosques. In short, the study of Islamic iconoclasm in this country, not to speak of the whole cradle of Hindu culture, has yet to make a meaningful start.

What we have proved beyond doubt is that destroying other people's places of worship and converting them into Muslim monuments is not only sanctioned but also prescribed by the tenents of Islam, the same way as reciting the *kalima,* doing *namāz,* paying *zakāt,* keeping *rozah,* and going on *hajj.* Anyone who says that Islam does not permit this practice is either ignorant of the creed, or has been deceived by Islamic apologetics developed in recent time. If a Muslim scholar or politician makes this statement, he is talking tongue-in-cheek, and stands exposed as a knave.

Appendix

WAS THE KA'BA A ŚIVA TEMPLE?

Some years ago I read an article proposing that the Ka'ba was a Śiva temple before it was converted into a mosque by Prophet Muhammad. The article cited a long hymn in Arabic addressed to Mahādeva who, according to the article, was the presiding deity of the Ka'ba. The hymn, it was stated, had been composed in the reign of Vikramāditya of Ujjain in the first century BC.

A friend who got interested tried to get the hymn traced to the extant collection of pre-Islamic Arab poetry. He approached several libraries abroad but drew a blank. He as well as I then dismissed the proposition as the product of that school of Hindu historians according to whom every building everywhere in the world was a Hindu monument at one time.

But in the course of the present study I have run into some facts which force me to revise my judgment. I am not yet prepared to say that the Ka'ba was a Śiva temple. I, however, cannot resist the conclusion that it was a hallowed place of Hindu pilgrimage. The facts are being placed before the readers for whatever worth they possess.

HINDU PRESENCE IN ARABIA

By now plenty of archaeological and literary evidence has come to light to show that Indian ports on the coasts of Tamil Nadu, Malabar, Maharashtra, Gujarat, Sindh, Baluchistan and Makran had participated since pre-Harappan times in the rich and vigorous trade carried on between China, Malaysia, Indonesia, Sri Lanka and India on the one hand, and Iran, Arabia, Ethiopia, Egypt, West Asia and Europe on the other. It is also known that agricultural, mineral and industrial products from India formed a major part of this trade. Colonies of Indian merchants existed all along the coasts of countries bordering on the Arabian Sea, the Persian Gulf, the Red Sea and the Mediterranean.[1] At the same time, colonies of Arabian, Iranian, Ethiopian, Egyptian, Syrian and European merchants had come up all along the aforementioned

[1] Shaikha Haya Ali Al Khalifa and Michael Rice (ed.), *Bahrain through the ages, the Archaeology*, London, 1986, pp. 73–75, 94–107, 376–82; Andre Wink, *Al-Hind: The Making of the Indo-Islamic World*, Vol. I, OUP, 1990, Chapters II and III; Lokesh Chandra *et. al.* (ed.), *India's Contribution to World Thought and Culture: A Vivekananda Commemoration Volume*, Madras, 1970, pp. 579–88; Muhammad Abdul Nayeem, *Prehistory and Protohistory of the Arabian Peninsula*, Vol. I, *Saudi Arabia*, Hyderabad (India), 1990, pp. 160–69.

coasts of India. The Arabs and the Ethiopians had a larger presence as compared to the rest.

Ibn Ishāq provides evidence that Hindu presence in Arabia on the eve of Islam was pretty strong. When Yemen was invaded by the Abyssinians, Sayf b. Dhū Yazan, a chief of the dominant Himayrite clan of Arabs, went to Chosroes (Khusrū), the king of Iran, for help. "He said: 'O King, ravens have taken possession of our country.' Chosroes asked, 'What ravens, Abyssinians or Sindhians ?' 'Abyssianians,' he replied."[2] Ravens meant blacks, who were identified with Indians and Abyssianans in the minds of Arabs and Iranians at that time. Later on, a deputation from B. al-Hārith waited on the Prophet. "When they came to the apostle he asked who the people who looked like Indians were, and he was told that they were the B. al-Hārith b. Ka'b."[3] The Prophet, it seems, was quite familiar with Indians.

In an article, 'An Image of Wadd: A Pre-Islamic Arabian God', Ch. Muhammad Ismail observed:

"The image of Wadd has been described by an Arab commentator as 'the figure of a tall man wearing a loin-cloth with another cloth over it, with a sword hanging round his neck and also with a bow and quiver: in front of him a lance, with a flag attached to it.' It will be perceived that this does not at all describe the figure in the Plate attached, which shows a short man wearing a kilt with pleats, like that of a Scottish Highlander. On the head is a close fitting cap with a long tassel, which seems to represent a long strand of hair. It may be noted that Beduins, who come to Aden from the Hinterland, while even to this day shaving the lower parts of the head with a razor, keep a tuft on the crown, and sometimes a long strand of hair like the *badi* of the Hindus. From this I once thought that perhaps there existed a connection between the peoples of Arabia and those of the Indus Valley, and I sent a drawing of this image of Wadd to Sir John Marshall, who wrote in reply as follows: 'I do not think that there is any connection between the kilted figure (from Arabia) and the Indus people. Kilts were worn at all ages, and this figure I should take to be some 2,500 years later than those from Mohenjo-daro'; that is to say, he dated it at about 800 BC."[4]

Archaeological excavations since the days of Sir John Marshall have, however, proved beyond doubt that there were regular contacts

[2] *Sīrat Rasūl Allāh,* op. cit., p. 30.

[3] Ibid., p. 646. *Tārīkh-i-Tabarī,* op. cit., p. 46, reports the Prophet as saying, *"Yēh tō Hindustānī ma'lūm hōtē hain."*

[4] *Indian Antiquary,* Vol. LVIII (May, 1929), pp. 91–92.

between Arabia and Sindh, even in the days of the Indus valley civilization. As we have seen, Sindh, Baluchistan, Makran, Fars, Islands in the Persian Gulf, and South Arabia were parts of the same cultural spread.

THE PAGAN ARAB PANTHEON

Prolonged contacts through trade and travel led to rich cultural contacts, particularly because Hindus as well as Arabs were Pagans, and neither of them harboured exclusivism characteristic of prophetic creeds. Some of the pre-Islamic Gods of Arabia, were like Hindu Gods. Students of comparative religion know that the pagan psyche, everywhere and always, has projected many similar forms and myths in respect of their divinities.

The Sabaeans of South Arabia in particular were well-known for transacting the richest trade with India. They had established colonies all along the western coast of India. They were sun-worshippers and had a famous sun-temple in their area. They believed in transmigration and the cycles of *yugas*. But what is most significant, "The Arabs gave the name Būdasp to the mythical founder of the religion of the Sabaeans..."[5] Būdasp was no other than the Bodhisattva. It seems that Buddhism had spread to South Arabia as Brahmanism had done earlier.

Coming to idols in Arabia, the worship most widely prevalent was that of Baal against whom the Bible and the Qur'ān hurl many invectives. Commenting on Qur'ān 37.123, Abdullah Yusuf Ali writes, "Both Ahab and Azariah were prone to lapse into the worship of Baal, the sun-god worshipped in Syria. That worship also included the worship of natural powers and procreative powers as in the Indian worship of the Lingam."[6] This is confirmed by W. Roberston Smith in his *Religion of the Ancient Semites*. He says that Baal was "symbolized in conical upright stones much like the *liṅga* of the Hindus" and represented "the male principle of reproduction."[7] Hindus present in Arabia could not but view Baal as the *Śivaliṅga*. Several such representations of Śiva must have been present among the idols in and around the Ka'ba, and many more in the Arabian sanctuaries elsewhere.

THE KA'BA

We have noted that the Ka'ba was a pagan temple crowded with idols and that the Islamic lore about its foundation by Abraham is pure

[5] *First Encyclopaedia of Islam,* op. cit., Vol. II, p. 770.

[6] *The Meaning of the Glorious Qur'ān,* Text, Translation and Commentary, Cairo, Third Edition, 1983, Vol. II, p. 1203, Footnote 4112.

[7] Summarised by Will Durant, op. cit., p. 309.

fiction. It should not, therefore, sound strange that Hindus present in Arabia took easily to worship in the Ka'ba. The pagan psyche responds with reverence to all idols, everywhere. The most popular Muslim historian, Firishta, writes, "Before the advent of Islam, the Brahmans of India were always going on pilgrimage to the Ka'ba, for the worship of the idols there."[8] He cites earlier historians as his authorities on the subject.

It is also significant that Muslims continued to believe for a long time that Lāt and Manāt, two prominent pre-Islamic Arab Goddesses, had fled from Arabia when the Prophet tried to destroy them, and taken refuge in the temple of Somnath. The repeated expeditions which Muslim invaders led in the direction of this temple were partly inspired by this legend which originated in Arabia. Why a legend about Somnath? Simply because its famous temple on the coast of Saurashtra was a place of pilgrimage for pagan Arabs, in the same way as the Ka'ba was for the Hindus. This inference may not sound unwarranted when we view the fact that Prabhas Patan was one of the principal ports for the Indian trade with Arabia, and had a strong Arab presence in pre-Islamic times. Arab presence in this port continued to be strong even in the post-Islamic period, down to the reign of the Vāghelās.

THE HINDU TRADITION

The Hindu tradition that the Ka'ba was a Śiva temple was very much alive in the days of Guru Nanak and is preserved in the *Janam Sākhīs*, particularly the *Makkē-Madīnē dī Goshatī*. It has to be investigated how far back in time the tradition goes. It cannot be said that it was invented by Guru Nanak.

Guru Nanak is reported to have said: "Mecca is an ancient place[9] of pilgrimage, and there is Liṅga of Mahādeva here. It was presided over by the Brāhmaṇas. One of the Brāhmaṇas, though born among them, became a Musalmān. He subverted the Atharvaveda and renamed it as Furqān. His own name was Muhammad which means the same as

[8] *Tārikh-i-Firishta* translated into Urdu, Nawal Kishore Press, Lucknow, 1933, Vol. II, p. 498 corresponding to p. 311 of the Persian text. The sentence in Urdu reads, *"Aur Brahman Hindustān kē qibl zahūr Islām khāna-i-Ka'ba kī ziyārat aur wāhaṅ kē butoṅ kī prastish kē wāstē hamēshah āmdo-shud kartē thē."* See also *Tārikh-i-Firishta*, translated into Urdu by Abd Illahi Khwaja, Deoband, 1983, Vol. II, p. 885; and John Briggs, op. cit., Vol. IV, p. 234. Briggs observes in a footnote, "The subject is full of interest, opens an extensive field of investigation for the Oriental antiquary, as leading to the development of the history of a period at which India and Egypt were closely connected..."

[9] *Makkē-Madīnē dī Goshatī*, edited by Dr. Kulwant Singh, Panjabi University, Patiala, 1988, p. 49.

Mahādeva.[10] He, however, vitiated all other names, so that Hindu names stood cancelled and Muslim names came into vogue[11].... All Brāhmaṇas were forced to fall away from the proper path, though they continued raising cries to Allāh. The Kalima says that God is one, but Muhammad got his own name mixed up with that of God. He sent out an order to the wide world that all should become Musalmāns. Most of those who were men of substance did not obey the order; but those who were tormented by want rallied round him. He concocted some sort of a creed, and taught it to them. They joined him for plundering the people; no one joined him with any other motive."[12]

There is no evidence as yet that the pre-Islamic Arabs were Hindus, or bore Hindu names, or knew the Atharvaveda, or were guided by Brāhmaṇas.[13] The *Janam Sākhī* seems to have preserved the Hindu refugee version of what happened in Arabia after the advent of Islam. It is on record in Muslim histories that Hindus resident in lands invaded by Islam had to run for their lives. The same thing had happened in the Roman Empire after it was taken over by Christianity.

The common people everywhere are prone to interpret events in the language of their own culture. It may be that by the time the story reached Guru Nanak, or perhaps much earlier, the Ka'ba had become a Śiva temple in the eyes of Hindus, and the principal idol there a *Śivaliṅga.* The pagan priests who presided in the Ka'ba became Brāhmaṇas, and the Qur'ān a perversion of the Atharvaveda. What is quite obvious is that the Hindus, resident or present, in Arabia did not relish the revolution that had upturned Arabia's ancient religion, and imposed a new belief-system by means of brute force. The image of the Prophet and his followers formed by Hindus at that time was more than confirmed by their subsequent experience of Islam in their own homeland. They had no reason to revise the story which has persisted till today, in spite of the herculean efforts made by a whole establishment to proclaim the Prophet as "a great religious teacher", and to whitewhash Islam into "a noble faith". In any case, the subject needs serious investigation by scholars in the field.

---

[10] By "Brāhmaṇas" Guru Nanak means the priestly class, *al-Ḥums* among the pagan Quraysh. Furqān, of course, is the Qur'ān. The word "Muhammad" in Arabic means "he who is prayed to".

[11] It is on record that the Prophet changed all personal names which referred to ancient Gods and Goddesses of Arabia, and substituted them with Jewish names. The practice continues till today in all conversions to Islam.

[12] Translated from a Hindi version of *Makkē-Madīnē dī Goshaṭī,* op. cit., p. 188.

[13] Though the *al-Ḥums* who looked after the Ka'ba in the pre-Islamic period resembled the Brāhmaṇas in many respects (*First Encyclopaedia of Islam,* op. cit., Vol III, p. 335).